The Property Tax and Alternative Local Taxes

Larry D. Schroeder
David L. Sjoquist

The Praeger Special Studies program—
utilizing the most modern and efficient book
production techniques and a selective
worldwide distribution network—makes
available to the academic, government, and
business communities significant, timely
research in U.S. and international economic, social, and political development.

The Property Tax and Alternative Local Taxes

An Economic Analysis

Praeger Publishers   New York   Washington   London

PRAEGER SPECIAL STUDIES IN U.S. ECONOMIC, SOCIAL, AND POLITICAL ISSUES

Library of Congress Cataloging in Publication Data

Schroeder, Larry D
    The property tax and alternative local taxes.

    (Praeger special studies in U. S. economic, social
and political issues)
    Bibliography: p.
    Includes indexes.
    1. Property tax—United States. 2. Local taxation—
United States. I. Sjoquist, David L. , joint author.
II. Title.
HJ4120.S34   336.2'2'0973   75-3751
ISBN 0-275-07480-3

PRAEGER PUBLISHERS
111 Fourth Avenue, New York, N.Y. 10003, U.S.A.

Published in the United States of America in 1975
by Praeger Publishers, Inc.

Printed in the United States of America

The fiscal plight of the large central cities has been a major topic of local public finance during the past decade. In response to these fiscal difficulties the National League of Cities (NLC), under a grant from the U. S. Department of Housing and Urban Development, undertook a "Local Finance Project." The purpose of the project was to analyze the nature of these fiscal difficulties and to explore a number of alternative proposals to deal with the problem. Case studies were conducted, in stages, in each of the 10 cities containing NLC-sponsored Urban Observatories. The third stage of the project, on which we worked, focused on the total and distributional effects of shifting the financial responsibility for providing government services from the central city to alternative levels of government. In the course of completing that project, we became increasingly interested in the specific issue of tax incidence on a local level. This interest culminated in this study of tax exporting and tax incidence.

An earlier version of this study was presented, in part, at the 1973 meetings of the Southern Economic Association. In addition to the financial assistance provided by the Department of Housing and Urban Development and the National League of Cities, the Bureau of Business and Economic Research at Georgia State University provided supplemental financial aid. We would also like to acknowledge the assistance provided by Frank Jozsa, Willis Sheftall, and Jerry DeFoor and the helpful comments on earlier drafts given by the members of the Urban-Public Finance Workshop at Georgia State University as well as the encouragement and aid provided by Roy Bahl.

The assistance of these individuals and agencies should in no way be construed as implying any concurrence with our conclusions or responsibility for any deficiencies that remain. Finally, we wish to thank Marilyn King and Jill Stanislawsky for their excellent typing of several drafts of the manuscript.

CONTENTS

LIST OF TABLES

The Property Tax and Alternative Local Taxes

During the latter part of 1974, Cleveland was planning to lay off 1,104 city employees; in Detroit the city budget analyst was projecting the largest revenue gap Detroit had ever faced; Chicago was planning to trim 598 persons from the civil service; policemen and firemen in Boston were seeking a 20 percent wage increase; New York was dismissing 1,510 city employees to reduce its $430 million budget deficit; and Philadelphia was cutting 562 employment positions.[1]

The above statements echo the scenarios that the mayors of major central cities have been describing for over a decade. Central cities in the larger metropolitan areas are in financial straits and are finding it increasingly difficult to balance their budgets; they are in what is commonly referred to as a "fiscal crisis."

Precisely how serious are the fiscal difficulties in which cities find themselves? What are the causes of these difficulties? What are the alternative solutions? These questions are the subjects of this chapter. With the problems and possible alternatives outlined, we turn in the remaining chapters to a detailed consideration of one of the possible remedies of the fiscal problems—the adoption of new taxes.

While the opening statements of this chapter suggest severe local fiscal problems, are cities in such a financial emergency that they are going bankrupt? Although defaults on municipal bonds during the 1960s did not come close to matching the number of defaults during the 1930s, there was a 250 percent increase in the number of defaults from the 1950s to the 1960s.[2] Despite this increase, a study by the Advisory Commission on Intergovernment Relations (ACIR) concluded that "in general, the present fiscal problems facing cities need not cause a financial emergency"; but the study did reveal that "several cities are facing trouble in maintaining balance in their operating budgets."[3]

While fiscal problems seem to abound for cities, the term "fiscal crisis" cannot be defined in economic terms. Instead, following Hirsch, it is more reasonable to define fiscal difficulties as a "large imbalance between people's aspirations for public services and their willingness and ability to pay for them."[4] That is, the financial difficulties in which central cities find themselves are the result of the interaction of two factors, expenditures and revenues, with desired expenditures increasing more rapidly than actual revenues. The consequence is either politically unpopular tax increases or unmet desires for public services.

Such phenomena should not be the exclusive domain of central cities; other governmental bodies would seemingly face the same divergence between desires and resources. Yet the focus of the problem is essentially a central-city problem. But the problem is a relative one, and, hence, in order to gain a perspective, we compare the financial condition of the central city with its suburban area.

Historically, per capita expenditures in the central cities have normally been higher than those in the suburban areas. The central cities were able to finance these higher service levels due to their relatively larger tax bases. Recently, however, the revenue bases, especially the property tax base, have grown at a much smaller rate than suburban tax bases, while at the same time the level of expenditures has been increasing at a faster rate within the central city. The combination of rapid increases in expenditures and relatively slower growth in the revenue-raising ability has made it increasingly difficult for central cities to balance their budgets at the existing service levels. To review the causes of these two-edged financial difficulties, we consider expenditures and revenues in turn.

EXPENDITURES

As has been well-documented in many studies of local government finance, total general expenditures by local jurisdictions have been increasing at a faster rate than has the gross national product (GNP). During the period 1960-71, the average annual growth rate of total direct general government expenditures for local governments was 9.7 percent compared with a growth rate for GNP of 6.9 percent.[5] Table 1.1 documents the point made above, that per capita expenditures in the central city not only are greater but also are increasing at a faster rate than those in suburban areas.

There are several possible reasons for the higher per capita expenditures in the central cities. These reasons may be summarized as reflecting either the higher cost of providing services in the central city or the greater "need" for services in the central city.

TABLE 1.1

Level in 1970 and Growth, 1957–70, of Local Government
Expenditures, of Selected Metropolitan Areas

Region and Standard Metropolitan Statistical Area	1970 Per Capita Total Expenditure (dollars)		Increase in Per Capita Expenditure, 1957–70 (percent)	
	Central City	Outside Central City	Central City	Outside Central City
Northeast				
Washington, D. C.	1,006	425	321	224
Baltimore	638	349	221	146
Boston	531	365	95	102
Newark	735	441	202	144
Paterson-Clifton-Passaic	381	418	146	124
Buffalo	528	520	174	148
New York City	894	644	248	148
Rochester	699	548	250	180
Philadelphia	495	325	200	136
Pittsburgh	450	309	139	141
Providence	392	265	145	168
Midwest				
Chicago	478	346	137	144
Indianapolis	355	306	99	186
Detroit	474	462	135	131
Minneapolis-St. Paul	540	520	192	177
Kansas City	485	347	161	210
St. Louis	463	292	211	135
Cincinnati	761	262	209	124
Cleveland	512	368	180	91
Columbus	398	290	140	86
Dayton	456	291	173	126
Milwaukee	562	486	145	131
South				
Miami	481	387	113	129
Tampa-St. Petersburg	372	289	134	225
Atlanta	554	315	251	215
Louisville	508	302	214	165
New Orleans	334	325	105	171
Dallas	352	279	91	158
Houston	305	307	97	64
San Antonio	252	288	123	177
West				
Los Angeles-Long Beach	624	529	134	161
San Bernardina	624	529	111	176
San Diego	484	472	153	150
San Francisco-Oakland	768	596	244	159
Denver	502	306	135	108
Portland	486	328	139	150
Seattle-Everett	524	471	201	232

Source: Seymour Sacks and John Callahan, "Central City-Suburban Fiscal Disparities in the 72 Largest Metropolitan Areas," in Advisory Commission on Intergovernmental Relations, City Financial Emergencies (Washington, D. C.: Government Printing Office, 1973), p. 123.

The first major factor related to higher costs of services in central cities is the environment in which city services are provided. Many studies for example have indicated that the greater population density in the city results in greater expenditures.[6] The higher density of persons and structures in the city make refuse collection and fire protection more costly. Crime rates within the city are higher, often necessitating greater expenditures on law enforcement. Schoolchildren tend to be from lower socioeconomic classes, making education more expensive.[7] Another factor that is frequently suggested as causing increased expenditures is commuters. A number of studies have attempted to determine whether or not suburbs "exploit" the central city—that is, whether the suburbanites who commute to the central city increase expenditures by more than the additional governmental revenue they generate. The results of these studies have not been conclusive, however.[8]

There are a number of factors related to the rate of increase in expenditures. First, the prices of goods purchased by local governments have been increasing 2.5 times as fast as prices of consumer products.* This of course applies to cities as well as suburbs.

Another major factor causing the increase in expenditures is the growth in local government employee compensation, which since the mid-1960s has outpaced the growth in employee compensation in manufacturing. One possible reason for this relative increase in compensation is the growth of public employee unions. Table 1.2 illustrates the increase in the number of work stoppages by public employees. Unionization activity has been concentrated within the central city and not the suburban areas, where efforts to unionize are more costly since there are fewer employees per government agency.

Regarding the "need" or demands for government services, many studies have noted that the greater the percentage of the population that is poor, aged, or young, the greater the demands for services such as welfare, health, and education. Since the central city has a greater percent of these socioeconomic groups than does the suburban areas, there are additional demands on city governments. In addition, the changing composition of city populations has increased the relative size of these classes within the central city. These increases account for a part, perhaps sizable, of the increase in the per capita expenditures within the city relative to the suburbs.

A final factor related to demands for expenditures is the increase in the public services provided, either increases in existing services

---

*Between 1968 and 1973 the GNP deflator for private consumption goods increased 24.7 percent while for state and local government purchases it increased 61.2 percent.

TABLE 1.2

Local Government Employees' Work Stoppages, 1958-70

Year	Number of Stoppages	Number of Workers Involved (thousands)	Man-Days Lost (thousands)	Workers Involved as Percentage of Total
1958-63 average	24	11.3	24.4	0.24
1964	37	22.5	67.7	0.40
1965	42	11.9	145.0	0.20
1966	133	102.0	449.0	1.70
1967	169	127.0	1,230.0	1.90
1968	235	190.9	2,492.8	2.70
1969	372	139.0	592.2	2.01
1970	386	168.9	1,330.5	2.36

Sources: U. S. Bureau of Labor Statistics, Work Stoppages in Government, 1958-68, Report 34 (1970), p. 9 and "Government Work Stoppages, 1960, 1969 and 1970" (1971; processed), p. 3.

or the addition of new ones.[9] For example, many cities have undertaken the collection of refuse, which still remains a private activity in many suburban areas. Some local governments have purchased the local mass transit agency and are now responsible for providing this service, which frequently operates at a deficit. In addition, cities have also expanded educational opportunities, for example, establishing community or junior colleges.

Making comparisons between areas regarding changes in particular services is difficult since the financial responsibility for public services differs between urban areas. For example, in some states the state government assumes a major responsibility for the financing of education while in other states education is primarily a local responsibility. However, Table 1.3 gives some indication of the rate of increase in particular services. Although welfare expenditures have increased at the fastest rate, they still comprise a small percent of the total local budget. Of greater importance is the increase in school expenditures, which have been increasing at a rate of 10 percent per year since 1960. About three-fourths of the increase in educational expenditures was due to increases in instructional costs per student as opposed to an increase in the student population.[10] The increases in per student expenditures are due in part to decreases in the pupil/teacher

TABLE 1.3

Change in Level and Distribution of
Local Government Expenditure in 78 Large SMSAs, 1962-72

Category	Percentage of 1962 Budget	Percentage of 1972 Budget	Percentage Change
Total direct general expenditures	100.0	100.0	178.4
Education	40.5	40.9	181.1
Highways	7.9	4.6	64.5
Public welfare	7.3	10.5	302.1
Health and hospitals	5.8	6.8	230.1
Police protection	5.6	5.7	182.9
Fire protection	3.3	2.8	135.3
Sewerage and sanitation	5.7	4.9	143.6
Parks and recreation	2.8	2.7	162.2
Financial administration and general control	2.8	3.5	152.1
Interest on general debt	3.9	3.9	179.2
Other	13.5	13.7	182.1

Source: U. S. Bureau of the Census, Local Government Finance
in Selected Metropolitan Areas and Large Counties: 1969-70 (1971);
and 1971-72 (1974).

ratio. However, 80 percent of the increase in instructional cost
per student is due to the increase in salaries.[11]

REVENUES

As indicated above, central cities generally have greater
fiscal capacity than do the suburban areas. However, central-city
expenditures per capita are so much greater than for the suburbs
that they outstrip their larger fiscal capacity. Further, the tax
bases within the central cities are growing at a slower rate than
in the suburban areas. For these reasons we find that there have
been changes in the level and composition of local revenue sources
in recent years. There has been a substantial increase in the amount
of expenditures financed through intergovernmental transfers and
a relative decline in the importance of the property tax, as governments have adopted alternative taxes. Despite this shifting away
from the property tax, it still remains the primary source of revenue

for local governments. In 1970-71, the property tax constituted
84.5 percent of all local tax revenue and 39.9 percent of all
general revenues, including intergovernmental grants.[12] Furthermore,
many individuals place much of the blame for the fiscal difficulties
of the central city on the property tax, which appears to be a major
factor in the fiscal difficulties central cities are experiencing.
Hence, we now turn to a more complete discussion of this particular
revenue source.

The property tax is a very unpopular tax, and politicians are
loathe to increase property tax rates. In the past few years, there
have been at least two national surveys that have elicited citizen
feelings regarding the property tax. ACIR reported that half of the
respondents to a survey it conducted felt that the property tax was
the worst or least fair of the major federal, state, and local taxes.[13]
Table 1.4 contains a summary of the results of the survey. There
were slight differences by age and location in the percentages
picking the property tax as the tax considered to be the least fair;
individuals over 60 years of age were more inclined to select the
property tax as the least fair than were younger individuals, and
a greater percentage of the individuals living in metro areas than
those living in rural areas selected the property tax as least fair.
On the other hand, 36 percent and 33 percent picked the federal
income tax and state sales tax, respectively, as the fairest tax.
When asked to select between a state income, a state sales, and
a state property tax as a means of raising additional revenue,
54 percent of those making a choice selected the sales tax, 29 percent
selected the income tax, while only 16 percent selected the property
tax.

Similar results were obtained by a survey conducted in 10 cities
throughout the Urban Observatory Network of the National League
of Cities.[14] When asked how they would prefer to raise additional
revenue for the city, 38 percent of the respondents selected the
sales tax, while only 11 percent selected the property tax.[15]

Further indirect indictment of the property tax is given by voter
referendums on school bond issues and by delinquent tax payments.
The percent of public school bond issues that have been approved
has fallen from 72.4 percent in 1962 to 46.7 percent in 1971.[16]
Of course, this decline may be due to factors besides the dislike
of the property tax—for example, rising interest rates and the
desire for reduced spending on education.[17]

Table 1.5 shows the current property tax collections as a percent
of current levy and the change in this percent from 1965 to 1970.
In an analysis of these data, the ACIR concluded that the level of
collection and changes in the level do not represent "any fiscal
deterioration in the cities with the possible exceptions of Pittsburgh
and Buffalo."[18] Column 3 of Table 1.5 shows the percentage
increase in city-purpose tax rates (that is, these do not contain

TABLE 1.4

Public Opinion on Taxes
(in percent)

	Which of the following would be the best way for your state government to raise taxes?			Which of the following is the fairest tax?				Which of the following is the least fair?			
	State Income Tax	State Sales Tax	State Property Tax	Federal Income Tax	State Income Tax	State Sales Tax	Local Property Tax	Federal Income Tax	State Income Tax	State Sales Tax	Local Property Tax
Total U. S. Public	25	46	14	36	11	33	7	19	13	13	45
18-29 years of age	29	38	23	39	13	30	8	22	13	15	41
30-39	46	47	14	31	13	36	9	22	16	15	40
40-49	25	49	10	43	10	30	5	19	12	12	46
50-59	20	50	11	33	11	39	8	17	14	14	45
60 or over	25	47	8	31	8	34	7	13	9	10	51
Under $5,000 family income	26	40	16	33	12	30	9	16	9	13	48
$5,000-6,999	21	46	18	37	11	32	7	18	11	14	44
$7,000-9,999	27	46	12	36	14	30	9	21	15	13	41
$10,000-14,999	26	49	11	34	10	38	6	22	15	14	41
$15,000 or over	23	51	13	40	8	36	7	19	13	14	46
Own home	25	51	9	34	10	26	8	19	12	12	47
Rent home	25	36	24	39	13	37	8	19	14	15	40
Rural	25	45	15	19	11	33	15	26	9	6	41
Metro (1 million and over)	26	42	16	39	10	30	7	15	13	14	45

<u>Note</u>: Other and don't know are not included.

<u>Source</u>: Advisory Commission on Intergovernmental Relations, <u>Financing Schools and Property Tax Relief</u> (Washington, D. C.: Government Printing Office, January 1973), pp. 162-65.

TABLE 1.5

Property Tax Levy, Collections, and Rates

City	(1) Property Tax Collections as Percent of Levy, 1970	(2) Change in Ratio of Collection to Levy, 1965-70	(3) Percentage Increase in Tax Rate, 1965-70
Phoenix	98.3	+0.9	0
Houston	91.7	+0.9	-10.0
San Diego	98.2	+0.7	-3.1
Detroit	97.8	+0.5	+12.1
San Antonio	90.6	+0.3	0
Denver	99.4	0	0
San Francisco	98.4	-0.2	+18.2
Kansas City	97.6	-0.2	+1.3
Cincinnati	97.5	-0.2	+2.6
Dallas	98.5	-0.6	+2.9
Seattle	96.9	-0.6	+5.0
Atlanta	94.1	-1.3	+33.5
Philadelphia	95.6	-1.7	+7.9
Nashville	96.0	-1.7	-10.4
Buffalo	96.8	-2.5	+24.1
Pittsburgh	94.0	-2.9	+44.8

Source: Advisory Commission on Intergovernmental Relations, City Financial Emergencies (Washington, D. C.: Government Printing Office, January 1972), pp. 51, 53.

increases for school systems). When we ran a linear regression between the values in columns 2 and 3 of Table 1.5, the results showed that the two variables are significantly and negatively correlated. Thus, the greater the increase in tax rates, the greater the decrease in the percentage of property tax levy actually collected. There are of course many different interpretations of this result; however, one interpretation is that the increases in the property tax rates are met with greater resistance to the extent that some individuals do not pay the tax.

What are the causes of the opposition to the property tax? As was noted above, individuals feel that the property tax is unfair. This, of course, implies many possible things. First, the assumed regressivity of the property tax is a major factor, especially for

lower-income individuals, influencing individuals' opinions
concerning the tax. Perhaps of more importance are perceived
horizontal inequities, as opposed to the vertical inequities. Since
the property tax is not self-administered, as is the income or sales
tax, it is difficult to maintain up-to-date records on the true value
of property. Even if property was assessed every year, errors
in the assessment process would lead to instances in which
property owners with the same-value housing pay different amounts
of taxes. There are of course difficulties for those who have
retired and no longer have substantial money income. This may
explain why those over 60 years of age express greater opposition
to the property tax (see above discussion). Two other difficulties
that influence citizens' opinions of the tax are that it is paid in
lump sum and that increases in the assessment, hence the tax
bill, occur in quantum amounts.[19]

The reluctance of city officials to increase the reliance upon
the property tax stems not only from citizen opposition but also
from other considerations. Many officials view the city as being
in competition for industry with other cities. Increases in the
property tax rate will, they believe, reduce the likelihood that
businesses will locate within their area.[20] Even worse in their
view is the possibility that existing businesses will leave. These
fears lead to a reluctance to increase property tax rates.

Another difficulty with the property tax as a revenue producer
is that, as noted above, the tax base grows slowly in an established
city—that is, a city that does not have undeveloped land within
its boundaries. Many studies have indicated that the income
elasticity of the property tax base is very low.[21] The study by
the ACIR of a sample of cities showed that between 1969 and 1970
their assessed values increased, but very slowly.[22] The average
(unweighted) of the percent increase for the sample of 29 cities
was only 5 percent. In another report ACIR presented the estimates
from various studies of income elasticities for selected taxes;[23]
the estimates are presented in Table 1.6. The elasticity of the
property tax is clearly lower than for the other taxes.

These considerations have caused political decision-makers
to become increasingly unwilling to rely upon the property tax as
the sole means of financing central-city expenditures. The result
has been an increased reliance upon other sources for additional
revenue.

PROPOSED REFORMS

There have been numerous proposals aimed at providing relief
from the property tax. One class of proposals calls for a reorganiza-

tion of governmental responsibilities. For example, Ruggles[24] and ACIR[25] propose transference of certain governmental functions to higher-level governments, with their larger tax bases. Other similar proposals include tax-base consolidation, such as that adopted in the Minneapolis-St. Paul metropolitan area, use of federal tax credits as advocated by the ACIR,[26] and reform of the property tax to reduce opposition.[27]

A second form of local property tax relief is the tapping of alternative revenue sources. Such sources include intergovernmental transfers, increased reliance on user fees, and alternative taxes. Although intergovernmental grants and user charges have been increasing in importance, exclusive reliance on these sources is quite unlikely, given the uncertainties attached to decisions made by higher governmental units and the possible inefficiencies, inequities, and administrative problems attached to user fees. For these reasons additional taxes appear to be necessary alternatives to the existing property tax in many metropolitan areas.

Numerous alternative taxes have, of course, been proposed, including selective excises of different types (for example, hotel/motel taxes, airport boarding fees, and liquor and cigarette taxes), general sales taxes, payroll taxes, taxes on incomes of persons and/or corporations, and general business taxes. Specific choice from among these alternatives evolves around political as well as economic considerations, for in all states the power to tax is granted only by the state government. Although such political decisions are of interest and are pragmatically important, economic considerations will play an important role in the final decision regarding which alternative revenue sources, if any, a local government will tap.

Probably of primary interest to decision-makers when considering this choice is the base of the proposed tax levy, for it is this base that determines either the necessary tax rate to obtain a desired revenue yield or the likely yield, given certain statutory rates. However, an important secondary bit of information in the choice process is the economic impact the tax will have on the residents of the locality—that is, it is important to know just how much of the tax yield will be derived from the local taxpayers (how much of the local tax is "exported" to nonresidents) and, secondly, for the portion of the yield not exported, how it is distributed across income groups. The questions of local tax exporting and incidence across income classes are the principal topics of this study.

THE SETTING OF THE CURRENT STUDY

The method employed in this study relies upon a two-sector general-equilibrium model. Using this model, along with certain

TABLE 1.6

Estimated Income Elasticities of Major State and Local Taxes

Investigator (Year)*	Area	Elasticity
Personal Income Tax		
Harris (1966)	Arkansas	2.4
ACIR (1971)	Kentucky	1.94
ACIR (1971)	New York	1.80
Harris (1966)	United States	1.8
Groves and Kahn (1952)	United States	1.75
Netzer (1961)	United States	1.7
ACIR (1971)	Hawaii	1.47
Planning Division (1971)	Arizona	1.30
Harris (1966)	New Mexico	1.3
Corporate Income Tax		
Peck (1969)	Indiana	1.44
ACIR (1971)	Kentucky	1.19
Harris (1966)	United States	1.16
ACIR (1971)	New York	1.13
Netzer (1961)	United States	1.1
ACIR (1971)	Hawaii	0.98
Planning Division (1971)	Arizona	0.97
ACIR (1971)	Oregon	0.93
ACIR (1971)	New Jersey	0.72
General Property Tax		
ACIR (1971)	New York City	1.41
Mushkin (1965)	United States	1.3
ACIR (1971)	Baltimore City	1.25
Netzer (1961)	United States	1.0
Bridges (1964)	United States	0.98
ACIR (1971)	Honolulu Co., Hawaii	0.89
ACIR (1971)	Multnomah Co., Ore.	0.84
McLoone (1961)	United States	0.8
Rafuse (1965)	United States	0.8
ACIR (1971)	Jefferson Co., Ky.	0.50
ACIR (1971)	Newark, N. J.	0.38
ACIR (1971)	Albany City, N. Y.	0.34
General Sales Tax		
Davies (1962)	Arkansas	1.27
Rafuse (1965)	United States	1.27
ACIR (1971)	Maryland	1.08
Peck (1969)	Indiana	1.04
Netzer (1961)	United States	1.0
Harris (1966)	United States	1.0
Davies (1962)	United States	1.0
ACIR (1971)	Kentucky	0.92
Planning Division (1971)	Arizona	0.87
Davies (1962)	Tennessee	0.80

NOTES TO TABLE 1.6

*Advisory Commission on Intergovernmental Relations, "State-Local Revenue Systems and Educational Finance," unpublished report to the President's Commission on School Finance, November 12, 1971; Arizona, Department of Economic Planning and Development, Planning Division, Arizona Intergovernmental Structure: A Financial View to 1980, Phoenix, 1971; Benjamin Bridges, Jr., "The Elasticity of the Property Tax Base: Some Cross-Section Estimates," Land Economics 40 (November 1964): 449-51; David G. Davies, "The Sensitivity of Consumption Taxes to Fluctuations in Income," National Tax Journal 15 (September 1962): 281-90; Harold M. Groves, and C. Harry Kahn, "The Stability of State and Local Tax Yields," American Economic Review 42 (March 1952): 87-102; Robert Harris, Income and Sales Taxes: The 1970 Outlook for States and Localities (Chicago: Council of State Governments, 1966); Eugene P. McLoone, "Effects of Tax Elasticities on the Financial Support of Education," unpublished Ph.D. dissertation, College of Education, University of Illinois, 1961; Selma Mushkin, Property Taxes: The 1970 Outlook (Chicago: Council of State Governments, 1965); Dick Netzer, "Financial Needs and Resources over the Next Decade," in Public Finances: Needs, Sources and Utilization (Princeton, N. J.: Princeton University Press, 1961); John E. Peck, "Financing State Expenditures in a Prospering Economy," Indiana Business Review 44 (July 1969): 7-15; Robert W. Rafuse, "Cyclical Behavior of State-Local Finances," in Richard A. Musgrave, ed., Essays in Fiscal Federalism (Washington: Brookings Institution, 1965).

Source: Advisory Commission on Intergovernmental Relations, State-Local Finances: Significant Features and Suggested Legislation (Washington, D. C.: Government Printing Office, 1972) p. 301.

specific assumptions, we obtain theoretical implications for the
incidence of tax burdens. Empirical estimates of both the exporting
and the incidence across income classes of tax burdens are then
generated for Atlanta, Georgia. The model and empirical methodology in this study are of sufficient generality to allow similar
studies for other metropolitan areas. Further, we feel that the
results of our analysis are applicable to many other cities, a
point we take up in Chapter 6.

The City of Atlanta provides a reasonable setting for pursuing
empirical estimation of the model presented. It is a major metropolitan area somewhat isolated geographically from other major
trade areas; thus, we avoid certain spillover problems in the
analysis. Further, the composition of Atlanta's population,
business, and industry is sufficiently heterogeneous to avoid any
special problems associated with a single dominating employer
within a city or reliance upon a single industry. Likewise,
Atlanta has experienced the common phenomena of flight to the
suburbs, office park construction, and erosion of the property
tax base via public construction.

Although the geographical makeup of Atlanta does not present
the major data problems created by many metropolitan areas—
for example, those encompassing two or more states—there are
sufficient quirks in the political jurisdictions to create a few
difficulties. The Atlanta standard metropolitan statistical area
(SMSA) in 1970 consisted of five counties, with the city itself
located primarily in Fulton County with a small proportion of
Atlanta's population (9 percent) residing in De Kalb County.
(The DeKalb County portion of Atlanta is primarily residential with
little business or industrial activity.) As will be seen in detail
below, the city relies quite heavily upon the property tax. Except
for business license taxes and certain selective excises, the property
tax currently is the only tax revenue source provided by state
statute. However, Atlanta, as well as other cities within Georgia,
has recently been pursuing additional taxing powers. Among the
taxes being proposed are the general sales tax (currently being
used by the public rapid transit system in Fulton and DeKalb
Counties at a 1 percent rate), selective excises on hotel/motel
rooms, and different types of income taxes, including taxes exclu-
sively on payrolls.

In the current study, we limit ourselves to consideration of
four tax types—the property tax, personal income tax, general
sales tax, and payroll tax. Fee arrangements were not considered
because of the reasons cited above, and other taxes, such as
the selective excise and business license taxes, were excluded
because of their relatively small base. Finally, corporate taxes
were not included because of the uncertainty attached to their
incidence and the administrative problems pertaining to location
of income sources, point of activity, and so on.

Chapter 2 of the study contains the model of local tax exporting, which focuses on three tax bases—capital and labor (both assessed at the site of use) and production in the locality. Chapter 3 begins with an empirical background regarding the observed base of each of four statutory taxes for the City of Atlanta as of 1970. In the latter portion of Chapter 3, the results of the theoretical model are applied to the tax-base estimates to derive estimates of exported taxes from Atlanta. Chapter 4 contains an outline of the methodology used in constructing a distribution of broad-based income for the city by family size. Chapter 5 provides the methods and results regarding the distribution of tax burdens by income class for each of the taxes under consideration. The final chapter summarizes the overall results of both the theoretical model and the empirical estimates obtained regarding tax exporting and incidence for Atlanta in 1970 and draws implications for other central cities.

NOTES

1. Atlanta Constitution, November 29, 1974, p. 1.
2. Advisory Commission on Intergovernmental Relations (ACIR), City Financial Emergencies: The Intergovernmental Dimension (Washington, D. C.: Government Printing Office, 1973), p. 10.
3. Ibid., p. 4
4. Werner Hirsch, "Fiscal Plight: Causes and Remedies" in Werner Hirsch, et al., Fiscal Pressures on the Central City (New York: Praeger Publishers, 1971), p. 4.
5. James Heilbrun, Urban Economics and Public Policy (New York: St. Martin's Press, 1974), p. 324.
6. See, for example, Harvey Brazer, City Expenditures in the United States (New York: National Bureau of Economic Research, 1959); and Roy Bahl, Metropolitan City Expenditures (Lexington: University of Kentucky Press, 1968).
7. This point has been made by Henry S. Terrell, "The Fiscal Impact of Nonwhites" in Hirsch, et al., op. cit., pp. 144-240.
8. See the discussion by Hirsch, op cit., pp. 19-20.
9. For an analysis of the increase in demand and increase in cost factors, see David Bradford, R. Malt, and Wallace Oates, "The Rising Cost of Local Public Services: Some Evidence and Reflections," National Tax Journal 22 (1969): 185-202.
10. Robert D. Reischauer and Robert W. Hartman, Reforming School Financing (Washington, D. C.: Brookings Institution, 1973), p. 18.
11. Ibid., p. 11.
12. Heilbrun, op. cit., p. 328.
13. ACIR, Financing Schools and Property Tax Relief: A State Responsibility (Washington, D. C.: Government Printing Office, 1973), pp. 162-65.

14. _Nation's Cities_ (August, 1971), pp. 10-22

15. Ibid., p. 15.

16. Reischauer and Hartman, op. cit., p. 22.

17. For a discussion of the latter point see Reischauer and Hartman, op. cit., p. 23.

18. ACIR, _City Financial Emergencies_, op. cit., p. 52.

19. For a discussion of the advantages and problems of the property tax, see C. Lowell Harriss, "Property Taxation: What's Good and What's Bad about It," _Journal of Economics and Sociology_ 33 (1974): 89-102.

20. For a discussion of the impact of taxes on the location of businesses, see John F. Due, "Studies in State-Local Tax Influences on Location of Industry," _National Tax Journal_ 15 (1961): 163-73.

21. For a discussion of these studies, see David Davies, "Financing Urban Functions and Services," in William F. Mitchell and Ingo Walter, eds., _State and Local Finance_ (New York: Ronald Press, 1970), pp. 302-31.

22. ACIR, _City Financial Emergencies_, op. cit., p. 52.

23. ACIR, _State-Local Finances: Significant Features and Suggested Legislation_ (Washington, D. C.: Government Printing Office, 1972), p. 301.

24. Richard Ruggles, "The Federal Government and Federalism," in Harvey Perloff and Richard Nathan, eds., _Revenue Sharing and the City_ (Baltimore: Johns Hopkins Press, 1968).

25. ACIR, _Urban America and the Federal System_ (Washington, D. C.: Government Printing Office, 1969).

26. ACIR, _Local Nonproperty Taxes and the Coordinating Role of the State_ (Washington, D. C.: Government Printing Office, 1961).

27. For a discussion of the possible reforms, see Dick Netzer, "Impact of the Property Tax: Its Economic Implications for Urban Problems," U. S. Congress, Joint Economic Committee and the National Commission on Urban Problems (Washington, D. C.: Government Printing Office, 1968).

The standard procedure in most tax incidence studies, and the one used here, is to employ a theoretical model to derive implications concerning the incidence of the various taxes considered. Until recently these studies of tax incidence have been exercises in partial-equilibrium analysis. Although general-equilibrium models have been used in international trade theory for many years, it was not until Harberger[1] published his paper on the incidence of the corporation income tax that formal general-equilibrium models found their way into tax incidence analysis.

In this chapter we briefly review these developments in tax incidence theory and then turn to the development of our theoretical model. Finally we consider the implications of the model used in Chapters 3 and 5 to estimate tax incidence.

TAX INCIDENCE THEORY

The basis of modern tax incidence theory[2] has its foundations in the work of Brown,[3] Rolph,[4] and Musgrave.[5] Previous to the work of these individuals, it was assumed that the burden of general sales tax falls upon prices and not on factor payments. Under the assumption that factor supplies are fixed, Brown concludes that a general sales tax must result in lower factor payments rather than higher prices. He argues that the conclusion that prices are increased as a result of a general sales tax is based on an improper application of partial equilibrium analysis. He notes that it makes no difference whether money wages fall and prices do not change or prices increase and money wages do not change.

Rolph follows Brown's lead to develop a theory that applies to any system of excise taxes. He draws the same conclusion as Brown with regard to a general sales tax. But Rolph extends the

analysis to consider partial excise taxes. He concludes that a
partial excise tax system results in some reallocation of resources
in favor of nontaxed sector, that the prices of taxed items rise and
the prices of nontaxed items fall, and that money income is reduced
by an amount equal to the yield of the tax. The latter result is
obtained since Rolph assumes that the excise tax revenue is held
by the government. Buchanan[6] argues that this assumption is
illogical since it implies that full employment will not be maintained,
whereas Rolph assumes that resources will also be fully utilized.

Musgrave, in building upon the previous work by Brown and
Rolph, notes that changes in the state of income distribution
result from changes in relative prices of factors and products
while the price level is set by monetary manipulation. This approach
avoids the question raised in the past regarding the effect of a
general sales tax on the price level. Musgrave agrees with the
conclusion of Brown and Rolph that a general sales tax, which
includes capital goods, is the same as a proportional income tax.
Unlike Brown and Rolph, however, Musgrave introduces the expenditure side of the budget and explicitly states the behavior of the
government in this respect.

The issues raised in the past have been made clear through
the work of Harberger,[7] Mieszkowski,[8] and McLure.[9] Until
Harberger's paper, discussions of tax incidence lacked a formal
general-equilibrium model in which the analysis of tax incidence
could be conducted. Harberger adopted the two-sector general-
equilibrium model from trade theory and applied it to an analysis of
the incidence of the corporation income tax. Harberger assumes
that there are two sectors within the economy, a corporate sector
and a noncorporate sector.

Each sector produces one aggregate product using capital and
labor. The two factors of production are assumed to be in fixed
supply and to be perfectly mobile between the two sectors. The
corporate income tax is treated as a tax on the use of capital
in the corporate sector. Harberger is then able to derive certain
theoretical implications concerning the incidence of the corporate
income tax. He concludes that the incidence of the tax between
capital and labor depends upon the relative values of a number of
variables such as the elasticity of demand, the elasticities of
substitution in production, and the capital-labor ratios in the two
sectors. Harberger then specifies values for these variables and
concludes that capital bears the burden of the corporation income
tax.

The two-sector general-equilibrium model has been extended
to other taxes and other situations. Mieszkowski[10] has extended
the model to an analysis of the differential incidence of other taxes
including general and partial commodity factor taxes. His approach
to the problem is the same as Harberger's except that Mieszkowski,

unlike Harberger, allows laborers and the owners of capital to have different expenditure patterns. This assumption means that the burden of a tax is the result of changes in relative factor prices as well as changes in relative product prices.

The two-sector general-equilibrium model has been extended and applied to a number of different situations. McLure[11] uses the model to develop a theory of the interregional incidence of regional taxes. McLure considers two sectors (or regions) that are isolated geographically but that participate in trade. He assumes that labor is perfectly immobile between the two regions but that capital is perfectly mobile. The remainder of the model is similar to that employed by Mieszkowski. Within the context of the model, McLure considers a number of different taxes. The burden of the tax is defined as the change in real income resulting from the change in relative factor prices and relative commodity prices. The interstate burden or incidence of the tax is thus defined as the change in the interstate distribution of income available for private use. His conclusions, like those of Harberger, depend upon the values of several variables. We will forgo a discussion of the conclusions since we are more interested in the methodology than in the results and since a discussion of the results would be rather lengthy.

Using the same model, McLure[12] has studied the locational impact of local tax policy. Instead of considering the changes in relative factor and product prices, McLure considered the effect on interstate capital flows induced by interstate tax differentials. Employing the same model as he did to analyze the interstate exporting of taxes, he determines the importance of various factors on the location decisions of capital owners.

A major difference, however, between this model and previous models is that perfect mobility and immobility of the two factors of production is not assumed. Instead McLure assumes that factors respond only partially to interstate differences in factor payments. This approach is extended to the theory of tax incidence in a later paper,[13] in which McLure concludes that the incidence results are quite different if factors are not perfectly mobile.

It is within the framework of the two-sector general-equilibrium model that we conduct our analysis.

THE GENERAL MODEL

The model we employ is similar to other general-equilibrium models used in the tax incidence literature; thus we only sketch the model and note the implications for the tax burden estimation presented in the next section. We leave the formal derivation of the mathematical expressions for the Appendix to this chapter.

We assume that there are two factors of production, capital and labor, denoted K and L respectively. Since we are dealing with an equilibrium model, it is implicit that the factors of production are fully employed at all times.

The work on the incidence of the corporation income tax assumed that both capital and labor were perfectly mobile between the corporate (taxed) sector and noncorporate (nontaxed) sector. It remains, however, an open empirical question as to whether capital or labor is more mobile geographically. We employ the assumption made by McLure,[14] that labor is perfectly immobile between regions while capital is perfectly mobile between regions.

Assuming that an SMSA constitutes a region, we assume that, between the SMSA and the rest of the United States, capital is perfectly mobile while labor is perfectly immobile. This clearly does not apply within an SMSA, where labor is mobile, given that residences do not have to change for labor to change employment. Therefore, we assume that capital is perfectly mobile within as well as into and from the SMSA and labor is perfectly mobile within and perfectly immobile into and out of the SMSA. We make the further assumption with regard to mobility that the residential locations of the owners of the factors of production are fixed. Thus a resident of Atlanta cannot change residency, but he can find work outside the city but within the SMSA.

These assumptions obviously are not realistic. A more precise approach would be to use factor mobility elasticities with values other than zero or infinity. The theoretical framework for such an analysis has been presented by McLure;[15] however, even if we were able to specify values for the elasticities, the empirical analysis in the following chapters would not have been possible using such a model.

The models that have been cited above consider two sectors—for example, two regions, one of which is the taxed sector and the other the nontaxed sector. Together the two sectors comprise the entire economy—that is, the union of the two sectors is assumed to be a closed economy. Since the City of Atlanta is the area over which the taxes are imposed, it is treated as one of the sectors of the model—that is, the taxed sector. But because of the mobility assumptions, we consider three regions: Atlanta, the rest of the SMSA, and the rest of the United States, denoted as sectors X, Y, and Z, respectively.

Since the Atlanta SMSA is small relative to the United States, we can think of the collective firms in the SMSA as one of a very large number of buyers of capital. Under such conditions we can assume that the market for capital is perfectly competitive so that the supply of capital to any one buyer (in this case the collective firms in the SMSA) is perfectly elastic. Thus, any action by the firms in the SMSA, whether increasing or decreasing the amount of capital used, has no effect upon the market price of capital. We therefore have a model in which there is a general equilibrium within the SMSA but only a partial equilibrium within the United States.

Let x, y, and z represent the aggregate output produced in sectors X, Y, and Z, respectively. Within the framework of the model, we consider a tax on the use of each of the two factors of production in sector X and a general tax on production in sector X.

The units of all inputs and outputs are defined so that all initial prices are equal to one. Since there are no money assets in the model, we treat z as the numeraire.*

We assume that the demand for the three products is unaffected by the distribution of income.[16] It follows that demand is solely a function of the price ratios—that is, there is no income effect—only a substitution effect. Although with three goods there are three price ratios, given any two of the price ratios, the third is determined. Hence, given the numeraire, demand for any product can be expressed in terms of the own and cross-elasticities. The demands for the three goods, however, are not independent, since once the level of demand for x and y is determined, the level of demand for z can be derived from the information given. Thus, we express demand for x and y as follows:

$$\frac{dx}{x} = -E_x(dP_x) + E_{xy}(dP_y) \tag{1}$$

$$\frac{dy}{y} = -E_y(dP_y) + E_{yx}(dP_x) \tag{2}$$

where E_x and E_y are the own price elasticities of demand for x and y respectively, E_{xy} and E_{yx} are the cross-elasticities of demand for x and y respectively,† P refers to price gross of direct taxes, and d is the derivative operator.

We assume that x and y are produced in industries that are perfectly competitive. We have no need for the production relations

---

*Since there are no money assets in the model, we cannot determine absolute prices, only relative prices. By treating z as the numeraire—that is, by assuming that its price is always $1, we are expressing all prices in terms of z. It would make no difference which of the products we labeled as the numeraire; the implications of the model would be the same.

†The own elasticity in this case refers to changes in the amount demanded relative to the change in ratio of the commodity's price to P_z. The cross-elasticity refers to changes in the ratio of the other commodity's price to P_z.

in sector Z, so they are not considered here. All firms in an industry
are assumed to be identical and to use both factors of production.
We assume that for each industry factors are combined according
to production functions that are homogeneous of degree one. The
production functions can be written in the following form:

$$\frac{dx}{x} = f_K \frac{dK_X}{K_X} + f_L \frac{dL_X}{L_X} \tag{3}$$

$$\frac{dy}{y} = g_K \frac{dK_Y}{K_Y} + g_L \frac{dL_Y}{L_Y} \tag{4}$$

where f_K and g_K are the capital–output ratios for the X and Y sectors,
respectively; f_L and g_L are the labor–output ratios for the X and Y
sectors, respectively; K_X and L_X are the amounts of capital and
labor allocated to the X sector; and K_Y and L_Y are the amounts of
capital and labor allocated to the Y sector. It also follows that
the substitutability of capital and labor in production can be written
as follows:

$$\frac{dK_X}{K_X} - \frac{dL_X}{L_X} = -S_x(T_K - dP_L - T_L) \tag{5}$$

$$\frac{dK_Y}{K_Y} - \frac{dL_Y}{L_Y} = -S_y(dP_L) \tag{6}$$

where S_x and S_y are the elasticities of substitution in production in
sectors X and Y, respectively; T_L and T_K are per-unit taxes on labor
and capital, respectively, in sector X; and where $dP_K = 0$ by
assumption.

We assume that factors are paid the value of their marginal
product. Hence, given that production functions are homogeneous
of degree one, it follows that the value of output is exactly
exhausted in payments to the factors of production. From this we
can write the change in prices of x and y as follows:

$$dP_x = f_K(T_K) + f_L(dP_L + T_L) + T_x \tag{7}$$

$$dP_y = g_L(dP_L) \tag{8}$$

where T_x is a per-unit tax on the production of x.

As assumed above, labor is perfectly mobile within the SMSA
and perfectly immobile between the SMSA and the United States and
capital is perfectly mobile throughout the United States. The supply
of labor to the SMSA is assumed to be perfectly inelastic, and thus
we can express the labor supply function as follows:

$$dL_X = -dL_Y \qquad (9)$$

Since we are interested in the effect of substituting other taxes for the property tax, we consider the differential burden of the various taxes.[17] However, in order to simplify the analysis, we assume that each of the taxes is replacing or is replaced by a neutral tax yielding the same amount of revenue. (A neutral tax is one for which product and factor prices are the same as they would be in the absence of the tax.) We assume that the composition of government spending does not change as a result of any changes in factor or product prices. Further, we assume that the benefits of government spending are unaffected by any change in real income.

The definition of tax burden that we employ is the same as that used by Musgrave,[18] McLure[19] and others—that is, the loss of income resulting from the reduction in factor payments resulting from reduced factor prices plus the loss of spending power resulting from changes in product prices. This measure of the burden is the loss from the sources of income side plus the loss from the uses of income side. As discussed by Friedlaender and Due,[20] such a measure of burden does not consider excess burden nor the loss of production resulting from reduced employment factors. Given the assumption that the supply of labor is perfectly inelastic and that $dP_K = 0$, and if we ignore the excess burden, it follows that the burden of a tax equals the tax revenue.

The burden of the tax, denoted B, is formally defined as follows:

$$B = (-dP_L\ L) + (dP_x\ x) + (dP_y\ y) \qquad (10)$$

where $L = L_x + L_y$. For Atlanta residents the tax burden denoted B_A, is given by the following:

$$B_A = (-dP_L\ L^A) + (dP_x\ x^A) + (dP_y\ y^A) \qquad (11)$$

where L^A is the labor force made up of Atlanta residents, and x^A and y^A are amounts of x and y, respectively, consumed by Atlanta residents.

To measure the burden, assumptions are made with regard to certain parameters of equations (1) – (9). We assume that S_x, S_y, E_x, and E_y all equal one.[21] and that E_{xy} and E_{yx} both equal zero.

Making these substitutions and solving the set of equations for dP_L, dP_x, and dP_y simultaneously yields the following:

$$dP_L = \frac{[-f_K(T_K-T_L) + f_K T_K + f_L T_L + T_x]\, L_X}{L} \qquad (12)$$

$$dP_x = f_K(T_K) + f_L(dP_L + T_L) + T_x \tag{13}$$

$$dP_y = g_L dP_L \tag{14}$$

IMPLICATIONS

If we set T_x and T_L equal to zero in equations (12), (13), and (14), it follows that $dP_L = 0$, $dP_y = 0$, and $dP_x = f_K T_K$. Thus, our model implies that a tax on capital used in the production of x is completely passed on to the consumer of commodity x. There is no change in the price of labor or in the price of commodity y.

A tax on L_X is borne by all labor in the SMSA (that is, Sector X plus Sector Y). Setting $T_K = T_x = 0$ in equation (12) we obtain the following:

$$dP_L = -\frac{T_L L_X}{L} \tag{15}$$

since $f_K + f_L = 1$.

Since labor in sectors X and Y are, by assumption, paid the same wage, it follows that the burden on the sources side is given by the following:

$$dP_L L = -\frac{T_L L_X}{L} L = -T_L L_X \tag{16}$$

which is equal to the tax receipts. However,

$$dP_x = f_L T_L (1 - \frac{L_X}{L})$$

$$dP_y = -g_L \frac{T_L L_X}{L} \tag{17}$$

Thus, the price of x increases and the price of y decreases. Individuals consuming x and y in the same proportion as they are produced experience no burden on the uses side. However, individuals who consume a disproportionate amount of x relative to y will experience a tax burden in addition to the burden on the sources (labor) side.

For the tax on production of x, the change in the price of labor is

$$dP_L = -\frac{L_X}{L} T_x \tag{18}$$

so that labor does not bear the whole burden of the tax. This is to be expected since a tax on the production of x is similar to a combined tax on labor and capital.

If the elasticities of demand were not equal to one, then our results obviously would be different. For example, if the demand for x were perfectly elastic so that the firms producing x could not adjust price without losing all their sales, then the tax burden on labor would be more than the tax revenue for T_K and T_x. If $dP_x = 0$, then for T_K,

$$dP_L \ L = -T_K \frac{K_X}{L_X} (L) \tag{19}$$

so that $dP_L \ L > T_K \ K_X$. Likewise, for T_x,

$$dP_L \ L = -T_x \frac{xL}{L_X} \tag{20}$$

so that $dP_L \ L > T_x x$. Since $dP_y < 0$, there is a net gain, or negative burden for consumers of commodity y.

Even if commodity x were produced and sold throughout the nation, implying a very elastic demand for the output of Sector X, there are still spatial effects such as transportation costs. Thus, firms in Sector X, given the absence of taxes and equal factor prices, have a cost advantage within some geographic area. If a tax is imposed in Sector X, the product price can increase without Sector X losing its entire market since there will still be a proportion of the market in which the local industry has a cost advantage.

APPENDIX: MATHEMATICAL DERIVATION OF EQUATIONS

In this Appendix, we formally derive the equations of the model for Sector X as presented in the text. The equations for Sector Y are derived in the same manner.

To generate the demand equations, consider the demand function for x, given by

$$x = D_x(P_x, P_y, P_z) \tag{A-1}$$

and assume that there is no effect on demand from changes in income. Take the total derivative of equation (A-1), note that $dP_z = 0$, and divide through by x to obtain

$$\frac{dx}{x} = \frac{\partial D_x}{\partial P_x} \frac{dP_x}{x} + \frac{\partial D_y}{\partial P_y} \frac{dP_y}{x} \tag{A-2}$$

Since $P_x = P_y = \$1$, it follows that the price elasticity of demand for x is given by

$$E_x = -\frac{\partial D_x}{\partial P_x x} \qquad\qquad\qquad\qquad (A\text{-}3)$$

and the cross-elasticity of demand for x is given by

$$E_{xy} = \frac{\partial D_x}{\partial P_y x} \qquad\qquad\qquad\qquad (A\text{-}4)$$

Thus equation (A-2) becomes

$$\frac{dx}{x} = E_x \; dP_x + E_{xy} \; dP_y \qquad\qquad\qquad (A\text{-}5)$$

Equation (A-5) is the demand equation in the text.

To derive the production relationships, assume the production function is given as

$$x = f(K_X, \; L_X) \qquad\qquad\qquad\qquad (A\text{-}6)$$

which is assumed to be homogeneous of degree one—that is, one that possesses constant returns to scale. From Euler's Theorem and the assumption that factors are paid the value of their marginal product, we know that

$$P_x x = P_L L_X + P_K K_X \qquad\qquad\qquad (A\text{-}7)$$

that is, the cost of the inputs equals the value of the output for a production function homogeneous of degree one. Noting that $P_x = \$1$, taking the total differential of equation (A-7), and dividing through by x yields

$$\frac{dx}{x} = P_L \frac{dL_X}{x} + P_K \frac{dK_X}{x} \qquad\qquad\qquad (A\text{-}8)$$

Equation (A-8) can be written as follows:

$$\frac{dx}{x} = \frac{P_L L_X}{x} \frac{dL_X}{L_X} + \frac{P_K K_X}{x} \frac{dK_X}{K_X} \qquad\qquad (A\text{-}9)$$

Since $P_x = \$1$, $\frac{P_L L_X}{x}$ is the share of the total output of x going to labor (since $P_L = \$1$, it is also the labor-output ratio) and $\frac{P_K K_X}{x}$ is the share of the total output of x going to capital (since $P_K = \$1$ it is also the capital-output ratio.) Thus, equation (A-9) can be written as

$$\frac{dx}{x} = f_L \frac{dL_X}{L_X} + f_K \frac{dK_X}{K_X} \qquad\qquad\qquad (A\text{-}10)$$

where f_L and f_K are the labor-output and capital-output ratio, respectively. Equation (A-10) is the same as equation (3) in the text.

The elasticity of substitution in production is defined as

$$S_X = - \frac{d(\frac{K_X}{L_X})}{(\frac{K_X}{L_X})} \bigg/ \frac{d(\frac{P_K}{P_L})}{(\frac{P_K}{P_L})} \tag{A-11}$$

Taking the derivative of the numerator of equation (A-11) we obtain

$$d(\frac{K_X}{L_X}) = \frac{dK_X(L_X) - dL_X(K_X)}{L_X^2} \tag{A-12}$$

or dividing by (K_X/L_X)

$$\frac{d(\frac{K_X}{L_X})}{(\frac{K_X}{L_X})} = \frac{dK_X}{K_X} - \frac{dL_X}{L_X} \tag{A-13}$$

Further, we assume that P_K and P_L are the prices of capital and labor net of tax on the two factors. Thus, the total effect for Sector X of imposing the tax on the factors is the change in the price of the factor plus the tax on the factors. Thus the denominator of equation (A-11), after differentiating it, becomes

$$d(\frac{P_K}{P_L}) = \frac{(dP_K + T_K) (P_L) - (P_K) (dP_L + T_L)}{P_L^2} \tag{A-14}$$

or

$$d(\frac{P_K}{P_L}) = dP_K + T_K - dP_L - T_L \tag{A-15}$$

since $P_K = P_L = \$1$. Thus, by combining equations (A-13) and (A-15), we have

$$\frac{dK_X}{K_X} - \frac{dL_X}{L_X} = -S_X(dP_K + T_K - dP_L - T_L) \tag{A-16}$$

which, when dP_K is set equal to zero, is the factor substitution equation.

Again, from Euler's Theorem we have

$$(P_x x) = (P_L + T_L) \, L_X + (P_K + T_K) \, K_X + T_x x \tag{A-17}$$

Dividing through by x we obtain

$$P_X = (P_L + T_L) \, \frac{L_X}{x} + (P_K + T_K) \, \frac{K_X}{x} + T_x \tag{A-18}$$

Now $L_X/x = f_L$ and $K_X/x = f_K$ so equation (A-18) becomes

$$P_X = f_L(P_L + T_L) + f_K(P_K + T_K) + T_x \tag{A-19}$$

Taking the total derivative of equation (A-19) yields

$$dP_X = f_L(dP_L + T_L) + f_K(dP_K + T_K) + T_x \tag{A-20}$$

since $dT_x = T_x$, $dT_L = T_L$, and $dT_K = T_K$ by assumption. Equation (A-20) is the same as equation (17) in the text.
Since

$$L = L_X + L_Y \tag{A-21}$$

and since $dL = 0$ by assumption, it follows that

$$dL_Y = - dL_X \tag{A-22}$$

which is the labor supply equation.

NOTES

1. Arnold Harberger, "The Incidence of the Corporation Income Tax," Journal of Political Economy 70 (1962): 214-40.

2. This literature has been reviewed by Peter Mieszkowski, "Tax Incidence Theory: The Effects of Taxes on the Distribution of Income," Journal of Economic Literature 7 (1969): 1103-24; Horst Recktenwald, Tax Incidence and Income Redistribution (Detroit: Wayne State University Press, 1971); and George Break, "The Incidence and Economic Effects of Taxation," in Alan Blinder et al., The Economics of Public Finance (Washington, D. C.: Brookings Institution, 1974), pp. 119-237.

3. Harry Brown, "The Incidence of a General Output or a General Sales Tax," Journal of Political Economy 47 (1939): 254-62.

4. Earl Rolph, "A Proposed Revision of Excise-Tax Theory," Journal of Political Economy 60 (1952): 102-17.

5. Richard Musgrave, "On Incidence," Journal of Political Economy 61 (1953): 306-23.

6. James Buchanan, Fiscal Theory and Political Economy (Durham: University of North Carolina Press, 1960).

7. Harberger, op. cit.

8. Peter Mieszkowski, "On the Theory of Tax Incidence," Journal of Political Economy 75 (1967): 250-62.

9. Charles McLure, "The Inter-Regional Incidence of General Regional Taxes," Public Finance/Finances Publiques 24 (1969): 457-83; "Taxation, Substitution and Industrial Location," Journal of Political Economy 78 (1971): 27-48; "The Theory of Tax Incidence with Imperfect Factor Mobility," Finanzarchiv 30 (1971): 250-62.

10. Mieszkowski, "On the Theory of Tax Incidence," op. cit.

11. McLure, "The Inter-Regional Incidence of General Regional Taxes," op. cit.

12. McLure, "Taxation, Substitution, and Industrial Location," op. cit.

13. McLure, "The Theory of Tax Incidence with Imperfect Factor Mobility," op. cit.

14. McLure, "The Inter-Regional Incidence of General Regional Taxes," op. cit.

15. McLure, "The Theory of Tax Incidence with Imperfect Factor Mobility," op. cit.

16. An alternative assumption is made by McLure, "The Inter-Regional Incidence of General Regional Taxes," op. cit. He assumes that all spending groups, including the government, have the same marginal propensity to spend and the same income-compensated elasticity of demand.

17. The alternatives to differential incidence are specific incidence and balanced-budget incidence. For a discussion see Richard Musgrave, The Theory of Public Finance (New York: McGraw-Hill, 1959), pp. 211-15.

18. Ibid.

19. McLure, "The Inter-Regional Incidence of General Regional Taxes," op. cit.

20. Ann Friedlaender and John Due, "Tax Burden, Excess Burden and Differential Incidence Burden," Public Finance/Finances Publiques 27 (1972): 312-23.

21. The assumption that the elasticity of substitution in production is one is not unreasonable given the empirical estimates of the parameter. For a discussion of the literature on capital-labor substitution in manufacturing, see Robert Lucas, "Labor-Capital Substitution in U. S. Manufacturing," in Arnold Harberger and Martin Bailey, The Taxation of Income from Capital (Washington, D. C.: Brookings Institution, 1969), pp. 223-74.

The model outlined in Chapter 2 is now used to estimate the amount of tax exporting for each of the taxes under consideration. We begin with a discussion and estimation of the various tax bases and then consider the procedures employed to estimate the tax exporting, examining each tax in turn.

ESTIMATION OF TAX BASES

Table 3.1 presents the tax bases as calculated and the tax rates necessary to yield $20 million in revenue. Since we want to compare the relative effects of the various taxes, it is necessary that tax yields be equal. The tax base estimates presented in this section are ex ante measures; no attempt was made to calculate the effect of the taxes upon the size of the tax base.

Property Tax

The value of the current (1970) property tax base is published by the City of Atlanta. The tax base presented in Table 3.1 includes the assessed value of tangible and intangible taxable property and the taxable value of public utilities, net of all homestead and personal property exemptions. This is the base used for the property tax.

In 1970 the revenue collected from the property tax by Atlanta for general government operation totaled $21.6 million, which was the basis for the choice of $20 million as the revenue collected from the alternative taxes. These figures were 36.9 percent of total general revenue and 66.3 percent of total taxes, not including business licenses and permits. These percentages are similar to

TABLE 3.1

Estimates of Tax Bases

Tax	Base (dollars)	Definition	Tax Rate	Annual Yield (dollars)
Property	1,918,753,121	Net assessed value of taxable property in Atlanta	$10.40 per $1000	20,000,000
Sales	2,691,981,259	Taxable sales in 1970 made in Atlanta	0.743 percent	20,000,000
Payroll	2,470,975,000	Wages and salaries of Atlanta residents and non-Atlantans working in Atlanta for 1970	0.81 percent	20,000,000
Add-on to the income tax	850,505,218	Net taxable Georgia income for Atlanta residents for 1970	2.35 percent	20,000,000
Income surtax	26,800,195	State income taxes paid by Atlanta residents for 1970	74.6 percent	20,000,000

Source: Compiled by the authors.

those for other governments in the United States, as noted in
Chapter 6. In 1970 the Atlanta School Board collected $46 million
from the property tax, which was 63 percent of total school revenue.
Within the property tax base, owner-occupied and rental housing
constitute only 36.4 percent of the base, a rather low percent
compared with other major metropolitan areas.

Payroll Tax

Of the taxes considered, the payroll tax is the only one that
is currently not being used by any governmental unit within Georgia.
Thus, unlike the other taxes, there is no obvious definition of the
tax base, making it necessary to select a definition from the various
alternatives. The base of the payroll tax is defined to include
all wages and salaries earned by residents of Atlanta regardless
of place of work and all wages and salaries earned in Atlanta by
nonresidents. The tax rate is assumed to apply to all payrolls
included in the base with no deductions or exemptions allowed.

One of the criticisms of such a payroll tax is that it excludes
certain types of income earned by Atlanta residents, such as
proprietor income, capital gains, interest, and dividends. Including
these items in the base would increase the base by about 15 percent
and result in a more progressive tax. Although it would be possible
to include these items in the base, it would be relatively easy to
avoid paying taxes on these items.

Since, as was noted above, the payroll tax is not currently
employed by any government in Georgia, there are no reported
figures on the tax base as there are for the other taxes. To estimate
the 1970 payroll tax base for Atlanta, we started with the amount
of wages and salaries received by Atlanta residents as reported
in the 1970 Census of Population.[1] To this figure we added an
estimate of the payroll paid to nonresidents working in Atlanta.
This estimate was obtained by taking the payroll for Fulton County
from the 1970 County Business Patterns[2] and allocating a proportion
to non-Atlanta residents working in Atlanta. To perform this
allocation we first assumed that the payroll for Fulton County is
allocated to labor working in Atlanta and in the remainder of Fulton
County in the same proportion as is the number employed. Assuming
that workers from outside the SMSA constitute the same proportion
of the Atlanta labor force as they are of the Fulton County labor
force, we used the 1970 Census of Population data on place of employment of SMSA residents to allocate a proportion of the County Business
Patterns payroll to Atlanta. The amount that was allocated to Atlanta
was then allocated between the residential and nonresidential components of the Atlanta labor force under the assumption that the Atlanta
payroll is divided between residential and nonresidential members of
the Atlanta labor force in the same proportion as is the labor force.

Equation (1) summarizes the computations that were made to estimate the Atlanta payroll tax base.

$$\text{PRTB}_A = \text{YL}^A + \left[\left(1 - \frac{N_A^A}{N_A}\right)\left(\frac{N_A}{N_F}\right)(\text{PR}_F)\right]\tag{1}$$

where

PRTB_A		estimated 1970 payroll tax base for Atlanta
YL^A	=	wages and salaries paid tó Atlanta residents (1970 <u>Census of Population</u>)
N_A^A	=	Atlanta residents who work in Atlanta (1970 <u>Census of Population</u>)
N_A	=	number of persons working in Atlanta who live in the Atlanta SMSA (1970 <u>Census of Population</u>)
N_F	=	number of persons working in Fulton County and who reside in Atlanta SMSA (1970 <u>Census of Population</u>)
PR_F	=	payroll for Fulton County including government payroll (1970 <u>County Business Patterns</u>)

In equation (1) the term $(N_A/N_F)(\text{PR}_F)$ is an estimate of the payroll paid in Atlanta, while the term $[1 - (N_A^A/N_A)]$ is an estimate of the percent of the Atlanta labor force that are nonresidents of Atlanta. The product of these two terms is an estimate of the Atlanta payroll paid to nonresidents. Notice that the term $(N_A/N_F)(\text{PR}_F)$ does not include the payroll of Atlanta residents who work outside of Atlanta (which is already included in YL^A). Hence, the term $(N_A/N_F)(\text{PR}_F)$ does not measure the complete tax base as defined.

Sales Tax

The sales tax base that is employed is the same as the current (1970) base for the Georgia state sales tax. (The Georgia sales tax applies to nearly all retail products, including food. Most services, including medical and financial services, are not included in the base.) It would be easy to change the size of the tax base by excluding or including certain items; however, any change in the base from that being used by the state would undoubtedly cause an increase in the cost of collection and enforcement. It was on this basis, as well as the availability of data, that we selected our sales tax base.

The Georgia Department of Revenue annually publishes, by county, the sales tax base implied by state sales tax receipts.[3] From the published amount for Fulton County for 1970 we allocated a proportion to Atlanta. This allocation was performed by first

determining, from the 1967 <u>Census of Business</u>,[4] the ratio of
retail sales plus selected service sales for Atlanta to the comparable
figure for Fulton County. The state estimate of the 1970 Fulton
County sales tax base was then multiplied by this ratio to obtain an
estimate of the 1970 Atlanta sales tax base. Equation (2) illustrates
the calculations.

$$ST_A = \frac{R_A + S_A}{R_F + S_F} \quad ST_F \tag{2}$$

where

ST_A = estimated 1970 sales tax base for Atlanta

R_A = retail sales for Atlanta (1967 <u>Census of Business</u>)

R_F = retail sales for Fulton County (1967 <u>Census of Business</u>)

S_A = selected service receipts for Atlanta (1967 <u>Census of Business</u>)

S_F = selected service receipts for Fulton County (1967 <u>Census of Business</u>)

ST_F = 1970 sales tax base for Fulton County (1971 <u>Statistical Report</u>, Georgia Department of Revenue)

Income Tax

Consideration was given to two simple types of local income
taxes, a local surtax on the existing (1970) Georgia income tax and
a local add-on to the existing (1970) Georgia income tax rates.
(Definitions for the Georgia income tax are similar to those for the
federal income tax.) Although other types of local income tax
structures are possible—for example, with the add-on tax the
percentage added could increase as income increases—the two
types of income taxes selected have a relative advantage in that
they are easy to administer.

The bases of both income taxes were derived from data provided
by the Georgia Department of Revenue,[5] which made available for
Fulton County, by adjusted gross income (AGI) classes, the number
of personal income tax returns, the average net taxable income,
and the average tax paid. To estimate the income tax base for
Atlanta, we first estimated the number of returns from Atlanta.
For this we assumed that the ratio of families in Atlanta to families
in Fulton County in the ith income class (income being measured
by census income) was the same as the ratio of the number of
returns from Atlanta to the number of returns from Fulton County
for the ith income class (income being measured by AGI). We then
multiplied the ratio of families by the number of returns from Fulton
County for each AGI class to obtain an estimate of the number of
returns from Atlanta from the ith AGI class. In other words,

$$R_A^i = \frac{f_A^i}{f_F^i} R_f^i \tag{3}$$

where R_A^i and R_F^i are the number of returns in the ith AGI class from
Atlanta and Fulton County, respectively, and f_A^i and f_F^i are the number
of families in the ith census income class in Atlanta and Fulton County,
respectively. (It is unclear whether an upward or downward bias
is introduced into the estimate of taxable income and taxes paid
from the use of the ratio of families by census income classes
applied to AGI classes.)

Assuming that the average net taxable income and average
tax paid for each AGI class are the same for Atlanta and Fulton
County, we multiplied the estimated number of returns from Atlanta
by the average net taxable income and by the average tax paid,
for each AGI class, to obtain the total net taxable income and
total income tax paid by Atlanta residents by AGI class. By summing
the net taxable income and taxes paid over all AGI classes, we
obtained the estimated bases for the add-on income tax and the
income surtax, respectively.

ESTIMATION OF THE AMOUNT OF TAX EXPORTING

In this section we utilize the model outlined in Chapter 2 to
measure the tax burden on Atlanta residents for each of the four
taxes.

In the theoretical analysis of tax burdens we assumed that
there are no other nonneutral taxes in the economy. However,
since local taxes are a deductible expense for individuals in
computing their federal income taxes, part of the tax paid to the
local government is offset by a reduction in federal income taxes.*
The effect of the tax offset is to reduce the burden of the local
tax on local residents and hence increase the amount of tax that
is exported.[6]

The tax offset applies to the statutory burden of the tax rather
than to the economic burden and, further, applies only for those
individuals who itemize their deductions in calculating their federal
income tax. For any individual the tax offset is determined by
multiplying the marginal tax rate times the increase in local taxes

_____

*If the federal government is assumed to collect a fixed amount
of revenue, then the tax rates for the federal government will have
to be increased as a result of the tax offset, thus negating part
of the offset. We will neglect these secondary effects. We also
neglect state income tax offsets, for reasons that will be explained
in Chapter 5.

paid by the individual. To determine the offset for all individuals
in any income class, it is necessary to find the proportion that
itemize their deductions. Finally, it is necessary to weight the
marginal tax rate for each income class by the proportion of the
total number of returns in each of the income classes. Since the
offset depends upon the levels of local taxes paid, the total amount
of tax offset for each tax varies as the incidence of the statutory
burden of the different taxes varies. The weighted marginal tax
rates are as follows: for the property tax—21.3 percent; for the
payroll tax—16 percent; for the sales tax—14.7 percent; for the
income surtax—21.3 percent; and for the add-on—18.4 percent.
A complete discussion of how these figures were obtained is
presented in Chapter 5.

Property Tax

From the data on national income for metropolitan areas
published in the Survey of Current Business,[7] we estimated the
value of the stock of capital in Atlanta. To estimate the value
of capital in Atlanta we multiplied estimated value-added by industry
sector (see Table 3.2) by $(1-f_I)$, the capital-output ratio. The sum
over all industry sectors equals $1213.15 million, which corresponds
very closely with the actual value of the nonresidential Atlanta
property tax base of $1219.64 million. Thus, we feel that the
treatment of the local property tax as a general tax on capital used
in production in Atlanta is an acceptable approach to the study
of the incidence of a local property tax.

The implication of the general-equilibrium model presented in
the previous chapter is that the property tax is borne by the consumers
of goods produced in Atlanta. From the model we know that the tax
burden, and hence the tax yield, equals $(dP_x)(x)$. By separating x
into its various component products, x_i, we can write

$$xP_x = \sum_{i=1}^{n} x_i P_{x_i} \tag{4}$$

By taking the total derivative of equation (4), we get

$$x dP_x = \sum_{i=1}^{n} x_i dP_{x_i} \tag{5}$$

To compute the tax burden on Atlanta residents, and hence the
extent of tax exporting, we had to determine the percent of each of
the x_i's consumed by Atlanta residents. The change in the price of
x_i is directly related to the amount of capital used to produce x_i.

For owner-occupied and rental housing, the property tax is, by
implication, borne by the occupant. This conclusion is the same as

TABLE 3.2

Payroll Tax Burden per Dollar of Payroll Tax,
Uses Side, Sector X

(1) Industry Sector	(2)[a] f_L	(3) dP_x	(4)[b] $(x + y)$ (millions of dollars)	(5) $\dfrac{x}{x + y}$	(6) (4)(5) x (millions of dollars)	(7) $\dfrac{xA}{x}$	(8) (6)(3)(7) $dP_x\ xA$ (millions of dollars)
Retail	0.6395	0.2373	949.42	0.7101	674.18	0.464	71.26
Wholesale	0.5676	0.2106	1,074.41	0.7113	764.23	0.186	29.94
Manufacturing	0.7771	0.2883	1,438.68	0.4177	600.94	0.186	32.22
Service	0.7068	0.2622	1,158.74	0.7849	909.50	0.464	110.65
Contract construction	0.8095	0.3003	391.60	0.5372	210.37	0.186	11.77
Transportation, communication, utilities	0.6730	0.2497	940.56	0.8056	757.72	0.186	35.19
Finance	0.2231	0.0828	1,864.63	0.7775	1,449.75	0.186	22.33
							313.36

[a]Employee compensation ÷ NNP: from U. S. National Income Accounts, Survey of Current Business, May 1971.

[b]Employee compensation in Atlanta SMSA ÷ f_L: from Survey of Current Business, May 1971.

Source: Compiled by the authors.

the assumption made in most burden studies, for example, McLure[8] and Musgrave et al.[9] The amount of housing available in the city will decline as a result of an increase in the property tax—that is, the amount of capital in the Atlanta housing market will decline. However, since the residential site for each individual is assumed fixed, no one will move to the suburbs even though the price of housing has fallen relative to the price in Atlanta.

The model also implies that the tax on commercial property is shifted to the consumer of these products in the form of higher prices. In the other tax burden studies there is no consensus as to the effect of the nonresidential portion of the property tax. Many of the studies split the burden of this portion of the tax between changes in the price of capital and the price of the product. When the industry is defined as "local," the general assumption made in these other studies is that the property tax is passed on to the consumer since presumably there is no outside competition. When the industry is defined as "national," so that presumably there is competition, owners of capital are assumed to bear at least a part of the tax. The definitions of local and national industries, however, vary from study to study.

Our objection to this type of analysis is that capital is mobile, so that it will not accept lower returns, whether it be a local or national industry. The price elasticity of demand may be different for a national vis-a-vis a local industry, so that the change in product price for any unit change in capital may be greater for the local than for the national industry, so that the extent of capital movements may be influenced by competitive conditions. However, this does not imply that the price of capital in one geographic area can change relative to the price of capital elsewhere. To imply otherwise means that capital is not mobile, an assumption we reject.

The first step in computing the amount of exporting of the property tax was to separate the property tax base into categories. On the basis of unpublished information provided by the Fulton County government,* we were able to determine the property tax base by selected categories. These data are presented in column two of Table 3.3.

Atlanta residents consume 100 percent of the owner-occupied and rental housing in Atlanta. Since the property tax paid on owner-occupied housing is an allowable deduction for the federal income tax, we applied the weighted marginal tax rate to the taxes paid on owner-occupied housing to obtain the federal tax offset, which is found in column (3) of Table 3.3. The tax offset is

---

*Fulton County acts as the property tax collection agency for the City of Atlanta.

TABLE 3.3

Property Tax Exporting

(1) Category	(2) 1970 Property Tax Base: Atlanta*	(3) Percent Exported
Owner-occupied housing	$ 415,657,880	21.3
Rental housing	283,451,869	0
Retail sales	181,789,139	53.6
Services	135,624,943	53.6
Utilities	155,937,547	95.0
Other	746,291,743	81.4
Total	1,918,753,121	47.8

*Calculated from unpublished data from Fulton County tax records.

Source: Compiled by the authors.

the only part of the residential portion of the property tax that is exported.

We obtained sales information from the three largest public utilities doing business in Atlanta—the gas, electric, and telephone companies. (The City of Atlanta supplies water to the area, and hence water supply is not treated as one of the public utilities.) On the basis of this information, we calculated that Atlanta residents in 1970 accounted for less than 5 percent of the total sales of these companies. We assumed that the property tax is passed on to all consumers that the utility serves, and hence it follows that 95 percent of the property tax on public utilities is exported.

We assumed that 53.6 percent of all retail and service sales in Atlanta are made to nonresidents. The value of annual (1970) retail and service sales (defined as items taxable under the state sales tax) in Atlanta has been previously estimated to be $2,692 million (see Table 3.1). The equivalent value for the SMSA is $4,530 million.[10] The Atlanta Chamber of Commerce estimates that the amount spent by conventioneers in the Atlanta SMSA in 1970 was $420 million,[11] 75 percent of which we assume was spent in the City of Atlanta. If all spending in the SMSA, net of convention spending, was by residents of the SMSA, the per capita spending in the SMSA would have been $2,956. (This assumption implies that our estimate of exporting is low, for it excludes all of the sales made to nonresidents of the SMSA.) We assumed that this was the value of per capita spending for Atlanta residents. We

further assumed that 87 percent of the purchases made by Atlantans
in the SMSA are made within the city. This figure is based upon
our estimate, or guess, that of the expenditures made by Atlanta
residents, 80 percent are made in the city and 92 percent are made
within the SMSA.[12] It follows from these assumptions that the
1970 expenditures in Atlanta made by Atlanta residents were
$1,249.1 million. This is 46.4 percent of the total sales made
in the city; in other words, we estimate that 53.6 percent of retail
and service sales are exported to nonresidents.

For the remaining categories in Table 3.3 we have even less
upon which to base our estimate of the tax exporting. From data
in the 1967 Census of Business, [13] we know that the amount of
wholesale sales per dollar of retail sales in 1967 in Atlanta was
$5.09 while for the United States it was $1.48. (Note that there
is double counting for wholesale sales since goods frequently
turn over more than once at the wholesale level.) Assuming that
for each $1 of retail sales in Atlanta there was $1.50 of (directly
related) wholesale sales, then it follows that about 70 percent
of wholesale sales were exported. Based upon the Survey of
Current Business[14] data on metropolitan area income, we find that
the wholesale sector constitutes about 40 percent of total income
excluding income from the retail, sercice, and real estate sectors.
Thus, the assumption we make that 60 percent of all the sales made
from the all-other category are exported is not unreasonable.
(Part of these products are shipped within the SMSA but outside
Atlanta. If these intermediate goods become part of the retail
sector in the rest of the SMSA, and given that Atlanta residents
purchase goods outside of Atlanta but within the SMSA, then this
should be calculated as a part of the burden. However, we neglect
this.) We assumed that the 40 percent that remains in the city
goes into the retail market. Since we have assumed that 53.6
percent of the retail market sales are exported, it follows that
53.6 percent of the 40 percent is also exported.

On the basis of these calculations we estimate that 47.8
percent of the property tax is exported (see Table 3.3). This figure
is high compared with the estimates obtained in other studies.
McLure[15] estimates that 16.5 of the property tax is exported from
Georgia. Brownlee[16] obtains an estimate of approximately 23 percent
for Minnesota, while Musgrave and Daicoff[17] estimate a value of
approximately 30 percent for Michigan. These are statewide studies
and therefore are not strictly comparable. The only study of tax
exporting for a local government with which we are familiar is the
New York study[18] in which it is estimated that 26 percent of the
property tax, exclusive of the tax offset, is exported. But
despite the difference between our figure and those of other studies,
we believe that our estimate is a conservative one.

To provide some feel for the robustness of our estimate, we recalculated the percentage exported, under the assumption that only 40 percent of retail and service sales and 65 percent of the all-other category are ultimately exported. Under these conditions, we obtained an estimate of 37.7 percent as the percent of the property tax exported. This figure is not substantially smaller than our original figure.

Payroll Tax

The payroll tax, unlike the property tax, affects the price of labor as well as the prices of both x and y. However, the payroll tax is borne entirely by labor in the sense that the tax burden on the sources side equals the tax revenue. The changes in the prices of the two aggregate products, however, affect the ultimate distribution of the tax burden. From equation (15) in Chapter 2, the change in the price of labor is given by

$$dP_L = -\frac{L_X}{L} T_L \tag{6}$$

that is, the net change in the wage rate equals the tax rate times the proportion of the total local labor force employed in the taxed sectors. Multiplying equation (6) by L, the total local labor force, yields $L_X T_L$, which is equal to the total tax revenue from the payroll tax on L_X. In other words, labor bears the entire tax.

The value of $P_L \cdot L$ is $3,928.04 million while the value of $P_L \cdot L_X$ is $2,470.98 million. The former figure is the 1970 SMSA payroll from the 1970 County Business Patterns,[19] while the latter figure is the estimate of the Atlanta payroll as calculated in the section of this chapter entitled "Estimation of Tax Bases." It follows from equation (6) that the wage rate for the SMSA falls by $0.629T_L$— that is, 62.9 percent of the tax per unit of labor. To calculate the burden on Atlanta residents we multiplied L^A, the amount of labor living in Atlanta, by $0.629T_L$. Thus, the tax burden on Atlanta residents on the sources side is given by

$$dP_L \cdot L^A = (0.629)T_L (1.23549 \text{ billion}) = \$777.12 \text{ (million)}T_L \tag{7}$$

The tax on labor is a tax on wages but not on fringe benefits. The price of labor, however, includes fringe benefits, and thus it appears necessary to include fringe benefits in the analysis. However, by assuming that fringe benefits are a constant percent β of the wage w, we can neglect fringe benefits. The price of labor P_L is equal to $w(1 + \beta) = \$1$. Consider a tax T_L' on all payments to labor such that the tax revenue equals the tax revenue from a tax just on wages, that is,

$$T_L' \left[w(1 + \beta) \right] L_x = T_L \, wL_x \tag{8}$$

Thus $T_L' (1 + \beta) = T_L$. The change in P_L is given by

$$dP_L = - \frac{L_x}{L} T_L' \quad - \frac{L_x}{L} \frac{T_L}{1 + \beta} \tag{9}$$

The loss of earning by Atlantans is then

$$dP_L(L^A) = - \frac{L_x}{L} T_L L^A \tag{10}$$

where L^A is the payroll for Atlantans. Equation (10) is the same as equation (7), and thus fringe benefits can be neglected.

Since payroll taxes are deductible in computing federal income taxes, we applied the weighted marginal tax rate to the payroll tax paid by Atlantans to obtain the tax offset. For the payroll tax, the tax offset rate is 16.0 percent, and, thus, the tax offset is given by

$$\text{Tax offset} = (0.160)(1,235.49 \text{ million}) T_L \quad 197.68 \text{ (million)} T_L \tag{11}$$

Next, we calculated the burden of the payroll tax on the uses side. For products produced in Sector X (Atlanta) we have from the model

$$dP_x = f_L(1 - \frac{L_x}{L}) T_L \tag{12}$$

where f_L is the labor-output ratio and L_x/L is 0.629, as calculated above. As with the property tax, we broke the aggregate output of Sector X into industry sectors, where the industry sectors correspond to those in the Survey of Current Business. They are listed in column (1) of Table 3.2. To measure the labor-output ratio, f_L, for each industry we calculated the ratio of labor income to net national product using national data by industry sector. (This assumes that the wage-rental ratio is the same throughout the nation and that the same technology is available everywhere. However, if there are tax differentials between regions, the wage-rental ratio will not be the same throughout the country.) The values of f_L by industry sector are listed in column (2) of Table 3.2. Using the expression for dP_x in equation (12), we determined the values of dP_x by industry sector, which are presented in column (3) of Table 3.2.

The same procedure was used to calculate the values of dP_y, except that the expression for dP_y is given by

$$dP_y = - g_L \left(\frac{L_x}{L}\right) T_L \tag{13}$$

For each industry sector, we assumed that g_L had the same value as f_L. The resulting values of dP_y are presented in column (3) of Table 3.4.

To calculate the burden on Atlanta residents resulting from the increase in the prices of x_i and the decrease in the prices of y_i, we had to find the values of x_i and y_i and the percentages of x_i and y_i consumed by Atlanta residents. To determine the value of x by industry sector, we first divided the value of employee compensation for the SMSA[20] by f_L for each of the industry sectors. This resulted in estimates of the value added by industry sector for the SMSA. These figures are presented in column (4) of Table 3.2. Next, it was necessary to disaggregate these figures between Atlanta and the rest of the SMSA. For the retail, wholesale, manufacturing, and service sectors, these allocations were made on the basis of the Census of Business or Census of Manufacturing payroll for Atlanta relative to that for the SMSA.[21] For contract construction, transportation, and finance, the allocations were made on the basis of the Fulton County (1970 County Business Patterns)[22] payroll relative to that for the SMSA, since there are no data on Atlanta payrolls available for these industry sectors. The allocations are presented in column (5) of Table 3.2 and the resulting figures for the value-added by sector for Atlanta and the rest of the SMSA are presented in column (6) of Table 3.2 and column (4) of Table 3.4, respectively.

We used the same allocators as we did with the property tax to measure the percent of the value added in each of the industry sectors in Sector X consumed by Atlanta residents. Thus, we assumed that 46.4 percent of the value added in the retail and service sectors was consumed by Atlanta residents and that 18.6 percent of the value added in the other sectors was ultimately consumed by Atlanta residents.[23] Column (8) of Table 3.2 gives the values of $dP_x \cdot x^A$ by industry sector, where x^A is the amount of x consumed by Atlanta residents.

As with Sector X, there is no direct information regarding the percent of the value added in any industry sector in Sector Y consumed by Atlantans. However, on the basis of previous assumptions, we were able to obtain an estimate of the percent of the value added in the retail and service sectors consumed by Atlantans. We previously calculated that the value of the expenditures made by Atlanta residents on items taxable under the sales tax is $1,561.35 million. From this, and the (previous) assumption that 80 percent of these expenditures are made in Atlanta and that 92 percent are made in the SMSA, it follows that the value of expenditures made by Atlantans outside Atlanta, but within the SMSA, is $124.91 million. This is 6.8 percent of the total value of taxable sales made within the SMSA outside Atlanta. Thus, we assume that 6.8 percent of the retail and service sales in Sector Y (the SMSA

TABLE 3.4

Payroll Tax Burden per Dollar of Payroll Tax,
Uses Side, Sector Y

(1) Industry Sector	(2)* g_L	(3) dP_y	(4) y (millions of dollars)	(5) $\frac{y_A}{y}$	(6) $dP_y \; y_A$ (3)(4)(5) (millions of dollars)
Retail	0.6395	−0.4022	275.24	0.068	− 7.53
Wholesale	0.5676	−0.3570	310.18	0.10	−11.07
Manufacturing	0.7771	−0.4888	837.74	0.10	−40.95
Service	0.7068	−0.4446	249.24	0.068	− 7.54
Contract construction	0.8095	−0.5092	181.23	0.10	− 9.23
Transportation, communication, and utilities	0.6730	−0.4233	182.84	0.10	− 7.74
Finance	0.2231	−0.1403	414.88	0.10	− 5.82
					−89.88

*From Survey of Current Business, May 1971.

Source: Compiled by the authors.

outside Atlanta) are made to Atlanta residents. For the Industry
sectors other than retail and service, we arbitrarily assume that
10 percent of the value added produced in Sector Y is imported to
Atlanta and consumed by Atlanta residents. The resulting values
for $dP_y \cdot y^A$ by industry sector are presented in column (6) of
Table 3.4, where y^A is the amount of y consumed by Atlanta
residents.

The total burden of the payroll tax on Atlanta residents, $B_A^T L$,
is given by

$$B_A^T L = - dP_L \ L^A + dP_x \ x^A + dP_y \ y^A - \text{tax offset} \tag{14}$$

The value of the various components of equation (14) are

$$dP_L \ L^A = - \$777.12 \ (\text{million})T_L \tag{15}$$

$$dP_x \ x^A = \$313.36 \ (\text{million})T_L \tag{16}$$

$$dP_y \ y^A = - \$89.88 \ (\text{million})T_L \tag{17}$$

$$\text{tax offset} = \$197.68 \ (\text{million})T_L \tag{18}$$

Thus, $B_A^T L$ equals $\$802.92$ (million)T_L, which is 32.4 percent of the
total payroll tax yield. Thus, we estimate that 67.6 percent of the
payroll tax is exported from Atlanta.

Sales Tax

In the model presented in Chapter 2, T_x is a tax on production,
or value added, in Sector X. A retail sales tax, however, is a
tax on the value added sold at retail in the taxing sector. Thus,
the value added in, say, manufacturing, in the taxed sector is
not all taxed; only that portion that goes to the retail market in
the taxing sector is actually taxed. Thus, a sales tax taxes the
value added in each industry sector at a rate dependent upon the
amount of the output eventually sold at retail in Sector X. In
addition, the sales tax taxes the value added of imported goods
that eventually are sold at retail in the taxing sector. However,
only a part of the imported value added is taxed since a part of
the imported product may be used in, say, manufacturing, and
then exported rather than being sold at retail. Thus, the sales
tax is a tax on all of the value added in the retail and service
industries of the taxing sector, on a part of the value added in
the other industries in the taxing sector, and on a part of the value
added imported to the taxing sector.

Let r represent the sum of all the value added from Sectors X
and Y that go into taxable retail and service sales in Sector X.

In other words, if 20 percent of the manufacturing value added in
Sector Y goes into the retail products sold in Atlanta, we would
count this as a part of r. The tax on the value added from outside
the SMSA that goes into the taxable retail and service sales is
not included in r, the reason for which will be apparent later.

The change in the price of labor within the SMSA is now given
by

$$dP_L = -\frac{L_r}{L} T_r \qquad (19)$$

where L_r is the amount of labor within the SMSA that goes into
the production of the value added included in the market value
of retail goods and services sold in Atlanta and T_r is the sales tax
rate. L_r is given by

$$L_r = \sum_i \alpha_i L_{X_i} + \sum_i \beta_i L_{Y_i} \qquad (20)$$

where the α_i and β_i are parameters indicating the fraction of the
output of the ith industry in Sectors X and Y, respectively, going
into the retail and service market in Atlanta, and where L_{X_i} and
and L_{Y_i} represent the amount of labor in the ith industry in Sectors
X and Y, respectively.

The change in the prices of x and y net of the tax are given,
respectively, by

$$dP_x = -f_L \left(\frac{L_r}{L}\right) T_r \qquad (21)$$

$$dP_y = -g_L \left(\frac{L_r}{L}\right) T_r \qquad (22)$$

The change in the after-tax price of the value added imported
from outside the SMSA that goes into the final retail and service
sales in Atlanta will simply be equal to the per unit sales tax.
The before-tax price of the product produced outside the SMSA is
the numeraire and by assumption does not change.

We are now in a position to explain how the burden of the
sales tax was estimated. In calculations for the payroll tax, we
estimated the value added by industry sector for Sectors X and Y.
Dividing these figures by f_L yielded an estimate of the value of
L_X and L_Y for each industry. The resulting values are presented
in columns (2) and (5) of Table 3.5. The values of α for the retail
and service industries are 1—that is, all the value added in the
retail and service industries in Atlanta goes into the taxable value
of retail and service sales. We previously assumed, in the discussion of the property tax, that 40 percent of the value added in

TABLE 3.5

Sales Tax Burden, Sources Side

(1) Industry Sector	(2) L_{x_i} (million)	(3) a_{ix}	(4) (2)(3) $L_{r_{xi}}$ (million)	(5) L_{yi} (million)	(6) b_{iy}	(7) (5)(6) $L_{r_{yi}}$ (million)
Retail	431.14	1.0	431.14	176.02	0	0
Wholesale	433.78	0.4	173.51	176.05	0.1	17.60
Services	642.83	1.0	642.83	176.16	0	0
Contract construction	170.29	0.4	68.12	146.70	0.1	14.67
Transportation, communication, utilities	509.94	0.4	203.98	123.05	0.1	12.30
Finance	323.44	0.4	129.38	92.56	0.1	9.26
Manufacturing	466.99	0.4	186.80	651.01	0.1	65.10
Total	2,978.41		1,835.76	1,541.55		118.93

Source: Compiled by the authors.

47

all of the other industries are ultimately sold at retail, and thus
the values of α for the other industries are 0.4. The values of β
for retail and service industries are zero since none of the retail
market in Sector Y is sold at retail in Sector X. For the other
industries, we have previously assumed a value for β of 0.1
(see the discussion of the payroll tax). The values of α and β
are presented in columns (3) and (6) of Table 3.5, while columns
(4) and (7) of that table contain the resulting values of $\alpha_i L_{X_i}$
and $\beta_i L_{Y_i}$.

The implied value of L_r is thus $1,954.69 million. This,
however, is the value of L_r for all retail and service sales, not
just those that are taxable. We assume that only 75 percent of
the retail and service sales are taxable; thus, the actual estimated
value of L_r that we used was $1,466.02 million. As was noted
above, P_L includes fringe benefits. Thus, we divided L_r by
payroll plus fringe benefits. The value of L is $4,998.77 million
and was obtained by taking the earnings for persons for the SMSA
from the Survey of Current Business[24] and subtracting military
earnings and proprietor income. To obtain the value of L^A,
$1,572.11 million, we multiplied the value of L by the ratio of
Atlanta payroll to the SMSA payroll. This calculation was based
on our previous assumption that fringe benefits are a constant
percent of payroll. Note that the sum of columns (2) and (5) of
Table 3.5 does not equal the value of L since the figures in Table 3.5
exclude the public sector.

The burden on the uses side is composed of two effects:
(1) a reduction in the prices of x and y resulting from the lower
price of labor and (2) an increase in price of r resulting from the
sales tax. The reduction in the prices of x and y, due to the fall
in P_L, and the resulting (negative) burden on Atlanta residents,
was calculated in the same manner as with the payroll tax—that is,
$dP_x = f_L dP_L$ and $dP_y = g_L dP_L$. The increase in price resulting from
the sales tax is just $r \cdot T_r$, where r is the taxable retail and service
sales and includes portions of x and y and imported z. The burden
on Atlanta residents resulting from $r \cdot T_r$ is $r^A \cdot T_r$ where r^A is
the sales to Atlanta residents. We previously calculated that
r^A/r has a value of 43.4 percent.

Given the data in Table 3.5, we calculated the values of
$dP_x \cdot x^A$, $dP_y \cdot y^A$, $r^A \cdot T_r$, and $dP_L \cdot L^A$, which are

$$dP_L \, L^A = -\$461.10 \text{ million } T_r \tag{23}$$

$$dP_x \, x^A = -\$150.05 \text{ million } T_r \tag{24}$$

$$dP_y \, y^A = -\$48.64 \text{ million } T_r \tag{25}$$

$$r^A \, T_r = \$1,249.08 \text{ million } T_r \tag{26}$$

tax offset $= \$183.11$ (million)T_r (27)

We applied the marginal tax rate of 14.8 percent to $r^A T_r$ to determine
the value of the tax offset, which is $183.11 million T_r.

The net burden on Atlanta residents from the sales tax was
therefore calculated to be $1,228.38 million T_r, which is 49.7
percent of the tax receipts. Thus, 50.3 percent of the sales tax
is exported.

Income Tax

The income tax is, by assumption, assumed to be borne
entirely by residents of Atlanta, and, thus, exporting of the income
tax consists only of the tax offset. Therefore, for the income
surtax, 21.3 percent is exported, while 18.4 percent of the add-on
tax is exported.

SUMMARY

In this chapter, we have presented our estimates of the tax bases
for the different taxes under consideration. The procedures and
results of the tax-exporting estimation are also presented. Table 3.6
contains the estimates of the extent of the tax exporting for the
various taxes.

TABLE 3.6

Estimates of Tax Exporting

Tax	Percent Exported
Property tax	47.8
Payroll tax	67.6
Sales tax	50.3
Income surtax	21.3
Income tax add-on	18.4

Source: Compiled by the authors.

The relative values of the figures are what might be expected,
a priori, given the assumptions and implications of the model. The

amount of the payroll tax that is exported is substantially greater than the amount for other taxes. This is to be expected given the large percent of non-Atlantans working within the city. There appears to be no significant difference between the sales and the property tax in terms of the amount of tax exported. Additional comments will be made in Chapter 6.

NOTES

1. U. S. Bureau of the Census, Census of Population and Housing: 1970, Census Tracts, Final Report PHC(1)-14, Atlanta, Ga., SMSA (Washington, D. C.: Government Printing Office, 1972).
2. U. S. Bureau of the Census, County Business Patterns: 1970, Georgia, (Washington, D. C.: Government Printing Office, 1971).
3. Georgia Department of Revenue, "1971 Statistical Report" (Atlanta; processed, 1971).
4. U. S. Bureau of the Census, Census of Business, 1967, vol. 2, Retail Trade—Area Statistics and vol. 5, Selected Service—Area Statistics (Washington, D. C.: Government Printing Office, 1970).
5. Georgia Department of Revenue, unpublished data sheets.
6. For a more extensive discussion of the tax offset, see Charles McLure, "The Interstate Exporting of State and Local Taxes: Estimates for 1962," National Tax Journal 20 (1969): 49-77.
7. U. S. Department of Commerce, Office of Business Economics, "Personal Income in Metropolitan and Non-Metropolitan Areas," Survey of Current Business 51 (1971).
8. McLure, op. cit.
9. Richard Musgrave et al., "Distribution of Tax Payments by Income Groups: A Case Study for 1948," National Tax Journal 4 (1951).
10. See Georgia Department of Revenue, "1971 Statistical Report," op. cit.
11. Atlanta Chamber of Commerce, Research Division, telephone conversation.
12. These figures were based, in part, upon the geographic distribution of shopping centers within the SMSA and our personal knowledge of the SMSA.
13. U. S. Bureau of the Census, Census of Business, 1967, vol. 4, Wholesale Trade—Area Statistics (Washington, D. C.: Government Printing Office, 1970).
14. U. S. Department of Commerce, op. cit.
15. McLure, op. cit., p. 65.
16. O. H. Brownlee, Estimated Distribution of Minnesota Taxes and Public Expenditure Benefits (Minneapolis: University of Minnesota Press, 1960), p. 22.

17. Richard Musgrave and Darwin Daicoff, "Who Pays the Michigan Tax," in Staff Papers, Michigan Tax Study (Lansing, 1958), p. 135.

18. Alan Donheiser, "The Incidence of the New York City Tax System," in Dick Netzer, Financing Government in New York City (New York: New York University School of Public Administration, 1966).

19. U. S. Bureau of the Census, County Business Patterns, op. cit.

20. U. S. Department of Commerce, op. cit.

21. U. S. Bureau of the Census, Census of Business, 1967, op. cit. and Census of Manufacturing, 1967, vol. 2, Area Statistics (Washington, D. C.: Government Printing Office, 1971).

22. U. S. Bureau of the Census, County Business Patterns, op. cit.

23. See the discussion of the property tax for an explanation of how these percentages were obtained.

24. U. S. Department of Commerce, op. cit.

4

CONSTRUCTION OF
A LOCAL INCOME
DISTRIBUTION

Prior to the estimation of tax incidence for residents of Atlanta, it is necessary to construct a distribution of income for city residents. This distribution should contain information on the source of income and on the distribution of income by family size, since the yields of the alternative taxes considered are functions of either one or both of these variables. As has been noted in numerous discussions of the distribution of income, money income may be an imperfect measure of the resources at the command of spending units. Thus, for burden measures, it is desirable to utilize a broad-based concept of income. In this chapter, we outline the basic procedures followed in constructing a distribution of broadly defined income by income source and family size for residents of the City of Atlanta in 1969.[1]

The most accessible source of income distribution data is, of course, the Census of Population and Housing. However, in addition to the definitional deficiencies alluded to above, these data suffer from underreporting. Thus, starting with the census data, it was necessary to adjust for underreporting, to include other non-census income sources, and finally to disaggregate the resulting distribution by family size. A fairly simple income construction method was used to accomplish these objectives.

The computation method relies upon seven basic steps, each of which is considered in separate sections below. The first three steps combine the census income data for the SMSA data on U. S. income distributions to derive an SMSA income distribution by class and source. Such a distribution is not presented in the census. In step 1, total census income in the SMSA for six income categories is determined and recategorized into four sources of income; in step 2, nationwide income data are used to estimate total income by class in the SMSA; and in step 3 information from steps 1 and 2 are combined with nationwide data and iterated to a distribution of income by class and source.

Step 4 is designed to account for underreporting of incomes and exclusions of three income sources—Other Labor Income, Imputed Rental Income, and Capital Gains Income. These adjustments yield a fully reported, broad-based distribution of income for the SMSA.

Step 5 separates central-city income from the result of step 4, yielding a distribution of income by source and class for residents of the city.

In distribution resulting from step 5, computed income class means can lie outside the class bounds. Thus, in step 6, income-receiving units are shifted to higher classes to account for the increased incomes resulting from the adjustments for underreporting and addition of excluded income sources.

Step 7 estimates a distribution of income in the city by family size. This distribution can then be combined with the results of step 6 to yield a single three-way distribution of income by family size, income source, and income class.

The last section summarizes the computational procedures and compares the resulting income distribution with the original census income distribution.

STEP 1: RECATEGORIZATION BY SOURCE OF CENSUS INCOME

The 1970 Census of Population provides information on six different categories of income: Wage and Salary, Self-Employment (non-farm), Self-Employment (farm), Social Security, Public Assistance, and Other.[2] For each income category, we determine from the census data[3] total income for families and for unrelated individuals.

The six income categories listed above are not compatible with certain data sources used below. Thus we redefine the six income categories into four income sources: (1) Wages and Salaries remains unaltered. (2) Self-Employment (non-farm) and Self-Employment (farm) are summed and called "Proprietor Income." (3) Social Security and Public Assistance income are summed and divided by 0.7108 to yield "Transfer Income." According to the Current Population Reports (CPR),[4] the national sum of Social Security and Public Assistance is 0.7108 of total transfer payments. Transfer payments in CPR include social security, public assistance, unemployment and workmen's compensation, government pensions, and veterans' payments. It is assumed that this ratio is the same for the Atlanta SMSA as for the nation. (4) Because of the desire to maintain integrity of the income totals, the amount by which the original sum of Social Security and Public Assistance is increased to become Transfer Income is subtracted from Other Income. (Other Income includes unemployment and workmen's

compensation, government pensions, and veterans' payments.)
We call the remainder "Property Income," since it is primarily
earned in the form of interest, dividends, and rental income.

These transformations result in total income by source for the
Atlanta SMSA and are shown in Table 4.1 for families and for
unrelated individuals.

TABLE 4.1

1969 Census Income for Atlanta SMSA by Category
(in dollars)

Category	(1) Family	(2) Unrelated Individuals	(3) Total
Wage-salary	3,620,056,005	424,377,527	4,044,433,532
Proprietor	337,345,593	24,274,295	361,622,888
Transfer	130,223,544	40,357,207	170,580,751
Property	218,684,511	50,957,153	269,641,664
Total	4,306,309,653	539,966,182	4,846,275,835

Source: U. S. Bureau of the Census, Census of Population,
1970 General Social and Economic Characteristics (Washington, D. C.:
Government Printing Office, 1972).

STEP 2: INCOME BY INCOME CLASS

Although the 1970 census provides information regarding the
number of families and unrelated individuals in the SMSA in each
of 15 census income classes,* there are no data regarding the
amounts received by units within each census income class. Step 2
thus estimates total income by income class for the SMSA.

To perform this estimation, it is assumed that the SMSA income
class means are the same as those for the nation. We compute total

---

*The bounds of these income classes are as follows: 0-999;
1,000-1,999; 2,000-2,999; 3,000-3,999; 4,000-4,999; 5,000-
5,999; 6,000-6,999; 7,000-7,999; 8,000-8,999; 9,000-9,999;
10,000-11,999; 12,000-14,999; 15,000-24,999; 25,000-49,999;
and 50,000 or more. In our analysis we aggregate the final two
classes to yield the open-ended class, 25,000 or more.

SMSA family income for each income class as the product of SMSA families in the income class by the nationwide mean income within the class, as reported in CPR, Table 1. (The CPR definition of income is the same as used in the decennial census.) Additionally, we make the assumption that the mean income within the class for unrelated individuals is identical to that for families in the United States, as found in CPR. Given this assumption, we calculate total income by class for unrelated individuals in the Atlanta SMSA.

STEP 3: DETERMINATION OF INCOME BY CLASS AND SOURCE

We now have estimates of total income arrayed by the four income sources as defined in step 1 and total income arrayed by income class as calculated in step 2. We now combine these two distributions to provide an estimate of the distribution of total income by class and source.

This is accomplished by adjusting national income distribution information to make it applicable to our problem and then using the resulting adjusted national data and combining it with the results of Steps 1 and 2 above in an iterative process to yield the desired family income distribution by income class and source.

To adjust national income distribution information, we estimate total U. S. family income by income class, using the data in Tables 1 and 2 of CPR. This information is then combined with the distributions of income by source for cumulative income classes as published in Table 5 of CPR to disaggregate the income amounts for the 14 income classes and 4 income sources. The result is a 14 x 4 matrix showing the proportion of total income from each income source as earned by the U. S. families in an income class.

Under the assumption that family incomes from each income source in the SMSA are distributed over income classes in the same way as they are distributed for the nation as a whole, we estimate incomes by class and source based on the local estimates shown in Table 4.1. This yields a 14/4 matrix of total incomes by income class and income source for families in the SMSA.

We then adjust the total estimated income by income class so as to equal total income by income source. With this adjustment, the totals across income classes by income source in the 14/4 matrix equal the SMSA incomes by source. However, the totals across income source for each income class in the matrix are not equal to the estimated and adjusted class totals. From this position we begin an iterative process adjusting the matrix entries for each income class by the ratio of class total to the sum of matrix entries for that class. This yields a new matrix for which the sums across income sources for each income class equal the respective income class control sums; however, the sum across income classes for each income type may not equal the appropriate income source

total. A second adjustment is then carried out such that a new
matrix is formed for which the sums across income classes equal
the income source control sums. However, now there is no certainty
that the sum across income sources for each income class equals
the appropriate row total. This is the same position from which we
started the iteration process, so the steps are carried out until
the sums across income sources for each income class of the
computed income matrix and the sums across income classes for
each income source of this matrix are both within 1 percent of the
respective class and source control totals. This results in a
14 x 4 matrix of family income for the SMSA by class and source.

For unrelated individuals we assume that income within an
income class is distributed over the four sources of income in
exactly the same way as is family income. Thus, using the U. S.
data from the CPR plus the local census information regarding
unrelated individuals, we carry out the steps outlined above
until the iteration stopping criteria are again satisfied.

STEP 4: ADJUSTMENT FOR UNDERREPORTING
AND INCOME EXCLUSION

Underreporting, either willfully or because of oversight, is a
potential problem when using survey data to ascertain income
distributions. The remedy for such underreporting errors was to
use the estimate of yearly SMSA income by source collected from
the payers of income and published by the Office of Business
Economics (OBE).[5] By comparing the estimated totals of income
paid (OBE data) with income received (census data), for the various
income sources, we can adjust the income calculated in the
previous section. We assume that the relative level of underreporting
within an income source remains constant over income classes and
is identical for families and unrelated individuals. For Atlanta
SMSA in 1969, we found the following underreporting ratios:
Wages and Salaries, 0.937; Proprietor Income, 1.117; Property
Income (excluding imputed rental income from the OBE amount),
0.740; and Transfer Income, 0.540.

The above adjustments account only for underreporting of
census incomes. We now broaden the census income definition
to include Other Labor Income, Imputed Rental Income,[6] and
Capital Gains.

Other Labor Income (primarily employer contributions to private
retirement programs) is obtained from the Survey of Current Business.[7]
We first allocate total Other Labor income between families and
unrelated individuals according to the proportion of total Wage
and Salary income received by families and unrelated individuals
as reported in the census. Next, each amount is allocated to

income classes in the same proportion as each income class wage and salary amount is to total wage and salaries.

The OBE Imputed Rental Income is allocated across the several income classes. Since the bulk of Imputed Rental Income is that from owner-occupied houses, we determine the proportion of total housing values owned by families in each income group employing data from the census.[8]

Since the Census Bureau[9] uses income classes that do not coincide with our 14 and since median housing values are given for each class, special procedures were designed to determine a set of ratios that approximate the proportion of total SMSA housing values attributable to each income class. The ratios are then used to allocate total Imputed Rental income across income classes. We then determine that, in the Atlanta SMSA, 91.9 percent of owner-occupied houses contain two or more persons while the remaining 8.1 percent are occupied by only one person. We assume that 91.9 percent of Imputed Rental Income in each income class was earned by families, with the remainder flowing to unrelated individuals.

The Bureau of the Census follows the Commerce Department's convention of excluding Capital Gains Income from the definition of income. For our purposes it would be desirable to include accrued capital gains. However, due to the nonavailability of data, we focus instead on estimation of realized capital gains.

To include realized capital gains, we utilize the Internal Revenue Service (IRS) publication, Statistics of Income: Individual Income Tax Returns,[10] which provides a national distribution of net capital gains by adjusted gross income (AGI) for joint and separate returns and total net capital gains reported by taxpayers residing within the metropolitan area. We first assumed that net capital gains consist only of net long-term gains. Second, AGI distributions are given by the IRS for both joint filers and separate returns. The distribution of Capital Gains Income for families was determined from the joint tax return AGI distribution. Third, as is shown by Gorman,[11] AGI has remained consistently around 87 percent of personal income as reported by OBE. We thus assume that 13 percent of the capital gains within any AGI income class should be in the next higher income class when income is defined according to the OBE definition.

Given these assumptions we can allocate Capital Gains Income across income classes. Total realized Capital Gains Income for the Atlanta SMSA is doubled and allocated between families and unrelated individuals in the same proportion as total Property Income accrued to families and unrelated individuals. Finally we adjust for the difference in income definitions in accordance with the assumption made above. The result is a distribution of Capital Gains Income across our income classes.

STEP 5: INCOME DISTRIBUTION FOR THE CITY

The data generated thus far are applicable for the entire
metropolitan area. However, since we are interested in the income
distribution for only the central city, we now disaggregate the
income distributions to obtain distributions for the City of Atlanta.

An iterative method, similar to the one described in step 3,
is employed to derive a distribution for the central city. The
resulting distribution of income reflects the differences in both
the size and source distribution between the city and the SMSA.
(Differences in these income distributions are significant. For
example, although only 29.5 percent of total SMSA family census
income is earned by City of Atlanta residents, 60 percent of all
families in the $0-1,000 income class reside in the city, and
64.2 percent of all Public Assistance Income in the SMSA is
received by city residents.)

Each SMSA income class total is multiplied by the proportion
of families in the SMSA that reside in the city to yield estimated
family income by class earned by city residents. These amounts
become the "class control sums" in the iterative process. The
same step is performed for unrelated individuals. Further, we
determine for families and for unrelated individuals the percent
of total SMSA income by (recategorized) source earned by city
residents. These percentages are used to allocate income source
totals to the central city, which then become the "source control
sums" in the iterative process.

We now have a distribution of central-city income by source
and a distribution by class. Since the source and class totals are
not equal, the class control sums are adjusted by multiplying each
class total by the ratio of the total of the source control sums to
the total of class control sums. The iterative process described
in step 3 is then applied to the matrices of SMSA incomes for
families and for unrelated individuals. This process yields income
distributions by size and source for families and for unrelated
individuals for the city.

STEP 6: SHIFTING TO NEW CLASSES

One of the results of adjusting for underreporting and inclusion
of additional income sources is to increase the mean of each income
class. Most of the newly computed means lie above the boundaries
of the income class. It is therefore necessary to shift income-
receiving units into higher income classes. This section briefly
outlines the methodology for this shifting.

For income classes lying between $0 and $15,000, we make
three assumptions. First, we assume that the units are distributed

rectangularly within the income class being considered. This
assumption allows one to determine the proportion of income units
lying above and below the original class mean. Second, we assume
that the entire distribution of income-receiving units has shifted
upward in the same proportion as has the new mean, relative to
the original mean. Third, we assume a uniform distribution of
income-receiving units above and below the original mean. From
these assumptions, relatively simple calculations determine the
number of income units to be shifted up one or more income classes.

Under the uniformity assumption, the mean of any income group
is simply the midpoint of that group. Further, since the shifting
is proportional, uniformity is maintained after shifting. By knowing
the bounds of the interval into which a portion of the class is
shifted, the new mean income for this group is simply the midpoint
of the interval. Total shifted income is, therefore, the product
of this mean and the number of units shifted.

Due to the large width of the $15,000-25,000 income class,
an alternative shifting method was devised. In place of the rectan-
gular distribution, we assumed that the probability density function
defining the distribution of income units lying in the class is
$f(x) = g - hx$ where x represents income-receiving units. From this
assumption, it is relatively simple to estimate the number of
income units and amount of income shifted into the 14th income
class.

After shifting for all classes is accomplished, the shifted
aggregate income is allocated across income sources. This
allocation is accomplished on the basis of the proportion, for each
class, of total income from each income source in the original
income class.

Finally, for each class we sum, by source, all of the income
shifted into and remaining in that class. Thus, the preshifting
distribution of income by source is taken into account in the post-
shifting distribution of income. The resulting distribution by
income class and source is given in Table 4.2 for Atlanta families.

STEP 7: ALLOCATING INCOME BY FAMILY SIZE

We now estimate how income within each income class is
distributed across family sizes since the various tax bases considered
are functions of family size. We have adequate data for single-
person families (unrelated individuals) so our only concern is
with families of two or more persons. The Census Bureau[12] provides
a tabulation of the number of families living in central-city
owner-occupied units as well as in renter-occupied units cross-
classified by number of persons (2, 3-4, 5, and 6 or more) and
by 10 income classes. We assume that the distribution of number

TABLE 4.2

Final Distribution of Family Income
by Type
for City of Atlanta
(in dollars)

Income Class*	(1) Wage-Salary	(2) Nonlabor Income	(3) Proprietor	(4) Property
0-1	43,545	2,412	0	16,388
1-2	48,931	2,710	0	18,415
2-3	937,229	51,915	104,755	393,385
3-4	2,809,990	155,652	345,934	1,205,328
4-5	4,734,880	262,276	612,701	1,936,465
5-6	10,479,262	580,470	1,210,897	3,592,033
6-7	20,551,754	1,138,409	2,076,701	5,411,846
7-8	33,606,075	1,861,517	2,949,748	5,449,545
8-9	40,710,847	2,255,067	2,840,258	4,846,951
9-10	43,427,514	2,405,550	2,620,492	4,090,157
10-12	108,244,530	5,995,913	5,438,191	8,444,729
12-15	157,138,691	3,704,273	6,996,173	8,136,023
15-25	364,946,235	20,215,210	19,680,571	22,768,375
>25	290,195,949	16,074,620	52,714,331	56,352,059
Total	1,077,875,433	59,705,995	97,590,752	122,661,701

(5) Imputed Rent	(6) Transfer	(7) Capital Gains	(8) Total
1,117,621	50,763	191,442	1,422,172
1,255,853	57,042	215,120	1,598,072
1,719,533	2,556,103	308,037	6,070,958
2,880,907	7,559,287	553,464	15,510,562
2,597,495	10,186,207	615,880	20,945,905
3,202,280	13,600,679	1,020,603	33,686,226
3,958,751	13,970,021	1,447,972	48,555,455
4,528,441	11,900,320	1,609,802	61,905,449
4,544,841	7,774,887	1,338,570	64,311,423
4,828,213	5,549,273	1,183,937	64,105,135
10,577,364	8,815,903	2,393,877	149,910,507
14,648,791	8,043,368	2,772,788	206,440,107
33,222,001	13,905,836	7,960,914	482,708,142
27,941,180	8,218,675	66,367,610	517,864,425
117,023,272	112,188,367	87,989,018	1,675,034,538

*The income classes are defined as $0-999; 1,000-1,999; 2,000-2,999. . . .

Source: Compiled by the authors.

of persons in housing units is identical to the distribution of family
sizes in the city. For completeness, we disaggregate family size
3-4. So as to maintain compatibility with the 14 income classes,
we disaggregate the combined income classes. This disaggregation
is accomplished by data published in the CPR together with the local
family size data.

Finally, families are shifted into higher income classes using
the results of the process outlined in step 6, so that the family
size distributions are applicable to the income distribution which
was computed there. The resulting matrix of family size distributions
is given in Table 4.3.

TABLE 4.3

Estimated Distribution of Family Size
by Income Class

| Income | Proportions by Family Size | | | | | Total Number |
Class	2	3	4	5	>6	Families
0-1	0.412	0.244	0.148	0.073	0.122	3,297
1-2	0.412	0.244	0.148	0.073	0.122	1,066
2-3	0.522	0.198	0.109	0.069	0.101	2,441
3-4	0.525	0.200	0.103	0.069	0.102	4,294
4-5	0.484	0.218	0.111	0.073	0.113	4,649
5-6	0.447	0.216	0.136	0.076	0.125	6,191
6-7	0.428	0.214	0.138	0.087	0.133	7,549
7-8	0.410	0.205	0.151	0.102	0.133	8,354
8-9	0.411	0.200	0.155	0.091	0.143	7,607
9-10	0.395	0.212	0.154	0.098	0.141	6,713
10-12	0.372	0.201	0.181	0.110	0.136	13,649
12-15	0.362	0.164	0.219	0.111	0.143	15,406
15-25	0.336	0.161	0.233	0.122	0.148	25,827
>25	0.323	0.190	0.226	0.142	0.119	12,248

Source: Compiled by the authors.

A size income distribution by both income source and family
size can easily be derived from Tables 4.2 and 4.3. We assume
that, within any given income class, the proportion of income
from any particular source is distributed across family sizes in
the same proportions as is total income within that income class.

IMPLICATIONS OF THE METHOD

The broad-based income distributions resulting from the method presented here is compared with the original Census income distributions for the City of Atlanta in 1969 in Table 4.4. Columns (1), (2), (5), and (6) of Table 4.4 contain the results from the method described above.

The most obvious effect of the broadening of the income definition is, of course, the increase in total income. Total family income is increased by 37.6 percent while total unrelated individual income is increased by 35.7 percent.

With respect to the total distribution of incomes we find that there is not a major impact on the shape of the distribution; all incomes and units are shifted upward. The proportions of total incomes earned by particular segments of the income-earning units do not differ substantially; however, the absolute levels of income for these proportions do increase greatly under the broader income definition.

To observe changes in a single measure of income inequality under the two alternative income concepts, Gini coefficients of concentration were computed for each of the four distributions shown in Table 4.4. The results, shown in the final row of that table, indicate that under the broader income concept, income concentration decreases slightly for families, thus implying that the effect of adjusting incomes of low-income families for under-reporting and including Imputed Rental Incomes more than offsets the increased incomes due to the inclusion of Capital Gains Income, which accrue primarily to the highest income class. A very slight increase in the Gini coefficient is found for unrelated individuals. However, when family incomes and unrelated individual incomes are aggregated into a single distribution, we find the Gini coefficient decreases from 0.4826 to 0.4668 when changing from the census to the broader income concept.

We therefore find that the results of this income-construction process yield distributions not unlike the original census distributions; however, the incomes estimated are likely to reflect more adequately the distribution of actual economic well-being within the population. Then, when the tax burden estimates are made in the following chapter, the relative changes over income classes will more accurately indicate the true distributional effects of the levies.

TABLE 4.4

Final Income Distribution Comparisons

City of Atlanta, 1970

Income Class (in thousands)	Family Income			
	(1) Census Units	(2) Census Income (dollars)	(3) Estimated Units	(4) Estimated Income (dollars)
0-1	4,701	239,751	3,301	1,422,172
1-2	5,621	8,667,582	1,066	1,598,072
2-3	6,011	14,871,214	2,442	6,070,958
3-4	7,415	25,848,690	4,293	15,510,562
4-5	8,085	36,180,375	4,645	20,945,905
5-6	8,008	43,699,656	6,196	33,686,226
6-7	7,985	51,391,460	7,568	48,555,455
7-8	8,576	63,916,928	8,359	61,905,449
8-9	8,167	68,953,981	7,611	64,311,423
9-10	7,214	68,150,658	6,706	64,105,135
10-12	12,152	132,165,152	13,644	149,910,507
12-15	12,888	171,152,640	15,401	206,440,107
15-25	15,632	285,815,488	25,845	482,708,142
>25	6,871	245,885,606	12,249	517,864,425
Total	119,326	1,216,939,181	119,326	1,675,034,538
Gini	0.4037		0.3843	

	Unrelated Individuals		
(5)	(6)	(7)	(8)
	Census		Estimated
Census	Income	Estimated	Income
Units	(dollars)	Units	(dollars)
15,369	783,819	14,982	915,556
12,282	18,938,844	3,941	6,762,585
7,040	17,416,960	8,944	22,648,125
6,102	21,271,572	4,941	17,191,888
5,531	24,751,225	6,016	26,717,874
4,694	25,615,158	5,468	29,881,712
4,740	30,506,540	5,140	33,266,617
3,489	26,003,517	4,667	35,055,922
2,669	22,534,367	3,195	27,191,879
1,519	14,349,993	2,395	22,682,631
2,033	22,110,908	3,228	34,948,516
1,408	18,698,240	2,474	33,059,121
1,465	26,786,060	2,154	40,320,130
580	20,755,880	1,376	63,633,308
68,921	290,523,183	68,921	394,276,864
	0.5352		0.5362

Source: Compiled by the authors.

NOTES

1. The precise details of the algorithms used are available in David L. Sjoquist and Larry D. Schroeder, "A Method for Constructing Distributions of Broad-Based Income for Metropolitan Areas and Central Cities," Working Paper No. 7374-04 (Atlanta: Department of Economics, Georgia State University, 1974).

2. Definitions of the terms from the census can be found in U. S. Bureau of the Census, 1970 Census Users' Guide (Washington, D. C.: Government Printing Office, 1970).

3. U. S. Bureau of the Census, Census of Population: 1970 General Social and Economic Characteristics, Final Report PC(1) (Washington, D. C.: Government Printing Office, 1972).

4. U. S. Bureau of the Census, Current Population Reports, Series P-60, No. 75, "Income in 1969 of Families and Persons in the United States" (Washington, D. C.: Government Printing Office, 1972).

5. An estimate of yearly income earned in each SMSA for different income sources in the May issue of the Survey of Current Business by the OBE; compare "Personal Income in Metropolitan and Nonmetropolitan Areas," Survey of Current Business 51 (May 1971): 16-32. By making estimates from payroll records, welfare rolls, and so on, these totals should be more accurate than the census totals, which require respondent recall of data and must cope with the desire not to divulge personal income data.

6. These data are available from the OBE of the Commerce Department, although they are not regularly published.

7. SCB, op. cit.

8. U. S. Bureau of the Census, Census of Housing: 1970 Metropolitan Housing Characteristics, Final Report HC(2) (Washington, D. C.: Government Printing Office, 1972).

9. Ibid.

10. Internal Revenue Service, Statistics of Income: 1969, Individual Income Tax Returns (Washington, D. C.: Government Printing Office, 1971).

11. John A. Gorman, "The Relationship Between Personal Income and Taxable Income," Survey of Current Business 50 (May 1970): 19-21.

12. Metropolitan Housing Characteristics, op. cit.

5

With the distribution of incomes constructed, it is now possible to consider the incidence of the several taxes under investigation; that is, we can now consider how the imposition of local taxes would change the local distribution of income. Thus, for each tax, we estimate the total burden (net of tax offsets and exported taxes) that would be paid by each income class and then observe the resulting effect upon the income distribution.

In Chapter 2, we noted that the tax burdens are composed of changes in the prices of particular goods and services, such as housing and items taxable under the sales tax, changes in the price of labor, and, for the income tax, changes in disposable income. For example, a tax on labor was shown to involve both changes in the wage rate as well as the price of goods and services. Thus, rather than directly considering the burden of each of the statutory taxes, we first estimated, by income class, the burdens resulting from the tax-induced changes in prices, wages, and disposable income. First, therefore, we outline the methods used to estimate, by income class, the statutory base for a tax on residential housing, on income, on consumption, and on labor income.

Next, we explain the method used to estimate federal income tax offsets by income class. Then there is a discussion of the measure of tax incidence used in this study and an examination of the empirical results obtained for the four statutory taxes being considered. The chapter concludes with a brief summary.

METHODS OF COMPUTING TAX BASES
BY INCOME CLASS

In this section we outline the methods used to estimate the bases by income class of a local tax on residential housing, income, consumption, and wages and salaries.

Residential Property Tax Base
by Income Class

Determination of the base, by income class, of a tax on
residential housing must either rely upon observed income/property
tax base tabulations or be derived via some estimation procedure.
In addition, the estimates must take into account any institutional
arrangements that tend to alter the income/property tax base relationship, such as circuit-breaker provisions, homestead exemptions,
or variations in assessment ratios. Before outlining the two
estimation methods we used to approximate the relationship
between income levels and the residential property tax base, we
will first discuss the several institutional arrangements holding
in Georgia that would affect the tax base.

Our estimates encompass the effects of three institutional
arrangements—assessment ratios, homestead exemptions, and
low-income housing. Under Georgia law the assessment ratio
in 1970 was to be 40 percent of "fair-market value." We obtained
information from the Georgia State Department of Revenue regarding
the assessed values and selling prices of transacted property in
Fulton County in 1971. These data revealed that the average
assessment ratio was 0.331 in Atlanta; however, there was also
a rather large standard deviation associated with this result.[1]
We have used this information in the estimates performed below.

Residents of owner-occupied housing are allowed a $2,000
homestead exemption that is deducted from the assessed value of
their property in determining the individual's tax base. We assumed
that all owner-occupiers take advantage of this provision in the
law. However, because of lack of adequate data, we disregarded
a second provision in the law, which allows an additional $2,000
homestead exemption to owner-occupiers 65 years of age or older
with incomes of less than $4,000.

In addition to these exemptions, which affect the distribution
of the tax base, public housing also decreases the residential
property tax base and thus its distribution across income classes.
We simply assumed that residents of public housing do not pay
any residential property tax. To incorporate this assumption in
the analysis, we utilized the findings of a study performed by
the Atlanta Regional Metropolitan Planning Commission[2] which
lists the various public housing programs in existence as of June
1970 and which includes data on the number of residents of public
housing in various income and rental classes. We assumed that
none of these renters bear any of the residential property tax
burden.

With those institutional arrangements and assumptions in
mind we now turn to a discussion of the two methods we utilized
in deriving estimates of housing values by income level. The

first relies on estimates of the income elasticity of demand for
housing while the second uses a more ad hoc approach to the
question employing housing value/income data published for the
city by the Census Bureau. We consider each in turn.

In a recent review of housing demand literature, deLeeuw
found that "estimates of the income elasticity of the demand for
housing range from 0.4 to 2.1."[3] Although deLeeuw attempted in
that article to reduce substantially that range of likely values,
subsequent investigations have indicated that no definitive consensus
has yet been reached concerning this empirical question. We, therefore, review briefly the arguments made by deLeeuw as well as his
more recent critics. We then report on the empirical evidence we
have gathered for the City of Atlanta. Finally, we indicate what
income elasticity values we used in our estimation of the base of
the residential property tax by income class.

Three reasons are provided by deLeeuw as to why previous
estimates of housing demand elasticities may have been biased.
One is that most studies used income concepts that exclude imputed
rental income to owners of owner-occupied housing, and, therefore,
these elasticity estimates are biased away from one. The second
weakness indicated by deLeeuw is that although demand for housing
really should relate quantity demanded to expenses per unit of time,
market values are most often used; therefore, such estimates should
be reduced by at least 15 percent. Finally, he cites that often no
account is taken of differences in prices of housing services among
areas covered within a cross-sectional study. Upon reviewing five
previous cross-section studies deLeeuw performs an analysis of
housing demand in 19 metropolitan areas in 1960 and ultimately
reaches the conclusions that ". . . the overall elasticity of rental
expenditure with respect to normal income appears to be in the
range of 0.8 to 1.0" and that ". . . the preponderance of cross-
section evidence supports an income elasticity for homeowners
moderately above 1.0. . . ."[4]

Since these conclusions were published, there have been at
least two additional contributions to the question of housing-demand
elasticities that deserve review. In four of the five studies reviewed
by deLeeuw as well as in his own empirical work, grouped observations on cross-sectional data were used to generate the results.
Maisel, Burnham, and Austin[5] argue that this use of grouped
observations may yield estimates of elasticities that are biased
and/or inefficient. Using ungrouped data, they obtain elasticity
estimates substantially below those obtained when medians of
grouped observations are employed. When the estimates are
corrected for exclusion of imputed rental income from the income
measure and when adjusted for biases in the sample, they obtain
". . . an estimated elasticity of 0.62 when using the disaggregated
data, well below deLeeuw's own estimates. . . ."[6]

The importance of the form of the data used appears to be substantiated in the results of a study performed by Carliner.[7] Using panel data in which movers were followed closely (a weakness of most other studies, as cited by deLeeuw), Carliner found income elasticities of demand ranging from 0.472 to 0.746, depending upon the specification of the demand function and the form of the income definition used. Income elasticities for rental housing were consistently near 0.5, using alternative income definitions and functional specifications.

So as to investigate further these differences in results with grouped data, we used 1970 census data for Atlanta to estimate income elasticities of demand for housing. Using weighted least-squares analysis (with the weights equal to the cell counts) of the cross-tabulated income/housing value data determined from the 1970 census[8] we found that, under the assumption of constant elasticity of demand, the income elasticity did not differ significantly from 1.0 at a 99 percent level of confidence. On the other hand, using the marginal totals from the same census table and unweighted least-squares regression of the log of housing value on the log of income, we derived an estimated elasticity of only 0.52.

Where does this review of the literature on the empirical relationship between housing values and incomes leave us? As is summarized in Table 5.1, previous findings do not suggest an unequivocal answer to this question. Therefore, for our purposes here we simply assume particular values of income elasticities of demand for housing. We first assume that the elasticity of demand for owner-occupied housing is 0.75. As indicated in the table, this is somewhat of a compromise assumption, but certainly well within the range of most probable estimates found recently. We assume for rental housing that the income elasticity of demand is 0.50, substantially smaller than deLeeuw's range of estimates but quite similar to the findings of Carliner. When presenting the incidence results below, we report on the findings of a test of the sensitivity of our results to these assumptions.

A five-step method was employed to estimate property tax base by income class using the above-discussed assumptions. (1) To estimate expected housing values by income class we substituted the ith income class mean, I_i, into the log-linear equation

$$\ln HV_i = a + b \ln I_i \tag{1}$$

where b is the assumed income elasticity of demand for housing, 0.50 for renters and 0.75 for owners, the parameter a was arbitrarily chosen, and income is from Table 4.4. (The reason for the arbitrary selection of a is made apparent in step 5 below.)

TABLE 5.1

Summary of Findings
in Selected Housing Demand Studies

Source	Income Elasticities	Type Data	Other Considerations
Lee (adjusted)	0.6 renters	Household	No attempt to follow movers; results using
	0.8 owners	Household	no other explanatory variables
deLeeuw	0.8-1.0 renters	Grouped	Corrected for income definition problems
	0.7-1.5 owners	Grouped	
Maisel et al	0.62 owners	Household	Shows bias of grouped observations
Carliner	0.49-0.75 owners	Panel of households	Followed movers; estimates with and
	0.41-0.52 renters		without demographic variables; various income definitions

Sources: T. N. Lee, "Housing and Permanent Income: Tests Based on a Three-Year Reinterview Survey," Review of Economics and Statistics 50 (1968): 480-90; F. deLeeuw, "The Demand for Housing: A Review of Cross-Section Evidence," Review of Economics and Statistics 53 (1971): 1-103; S. J. Maisel, J. B. Burnham, and J. S. Austin, "The Demand for Housing: A Comment," Review of Economics and Statistics 53 (1971): 410-13; G. Carliner, "Income Elasticity of Housing Demand," Review of Economics and Statistics 55 (1973): 528-32.

(2) We then multiplied HV_i by 0.331, the assumed assessment ratio, to obtain expected assessed values for each income class.
(3) For net assessed values of owner-occupied housing we subtracted $2,000 from assessed values to account for the homestead exemption provision of the tax. (4) We then multiplied the net assessed owner and renter values for each income class by the number of owners and renters (net of public housing residents) in the income class, as determined from the 1970 Census of Housing[9] and adjusted to correspond with the income concept used here. This yielded total assessed values by income class for owners and for renters. These results were then aggregated over all income classes. (5) We compared the estimated total tax base for owner-occupied housing

and rental housing with the estimates of these bases as shown above
in Chapter 3 ($415,657,880 for owner-occupied and $203,451,869
for rental housing). At this point, we determined if the arbitrary
value chosen for parameter a in equation (1) needed to be adjusted
upward or downward to yield estimated net residential property
tax bases by income classes, which equaled the estimated total
base. For our data the resulting housing value estimating equations
are as follows:

$$\ln HV_i = 2.88 + 0.75 \ \ln I_i \qquad \text{for owners} \qquad (2)$$

$$\ln HV_i = 4.39 + 0.5 \ \ln I_i \qquad \text{for renters} \qquad (3)$$

The resulting mean housing value estimates appear in Table 5.2.
   From the aggregate tax base, a constant average tax rate can
be determined that would yield any desired level of residential
property tax revenues. This rate times the income class residential
property tax base then yields estimates of taxes for each income
group.
   The alternative method of estimating the tax base by income
class relies directly upon the cross-tabulations of income levels
by housing values reported in the Census Bureau, Metropolitan
Housing Characteristics.[10] Given the number of owner-occupied
housing units by the income class of the owners and the estimated
value class of the housing unit, it is simple to estimate the total
value of housing in the city by multiplying the assumed class marks
by the number of units classified in the value range. Upon
adjusting these values by the institutional arrangements discussed
previously and upon shifting the income units in the same way
described in Chapter 4, one can aggregate overall housing values
within an income class and determine a distribution of the tax
base over income classes. A similar method can be used on rental
values by income classes, also published in Metropolitan Housing
Characteristics, to derive a distribution of rents by income class
and then assume that the property tax base applicable to rental
housing is proportional to this distribution.
   Before elaborating on this second estimation procedure, several
assumptions should be made explicit. First, under this approach,
we are assuming that there is no consistent bias in the reporting
of housing values and incomes to the Census Bureau. More
importantly, we are assuming for rental housing that there is no
rental/value ratio difference over income classes. As Peterson[11]
has shown, this assumption may not be valid; instead it is more
likely that rental/value ratios decline as rents, and thus incomes,
increase. This can lead to less regressive (more progressive)
property taxes.

TABLE 5.2

Estimated Owner-Occupied
and Rental Mean Housing Values
by Income Class

Income* Class	Owner-Occupiers (dollars)	Rental (dollars)
0-1	130	215
1-2	2,213	2,182
2-3	3,484	3,164
3-4	5,061	4,294
4-5	6,538	5,294
5-6	8,136	6,332
6-7	9,786	7,364
7-8	11,464	8,382
8-9	13,210	9,413
9-10	15,036	10,465
10-12	17,527	11,864
12-15	21,869	14,218
15-25	31,553	19,192
≥ 25	78,250	40,350

*Income classes are defined as 0-$999; $1,000-1,999; $2,000-
2,999, . . .

Source: Compiled by the authors.

A multistep method was also used when employing the census
matrix of housing values by income classes. For owner-occupiers,
a three-step process was used. (1) The counts of housing units
by income and value class were multiplied by the appropriate class
mark for each value class and aggregated over the entire matrix.
This resulted in an estimated gross housing value for the city of
$1.38 billion. (2) Since the product of this gross amount times
the assessment ratio assumed above, 0.331, minus the $2,000
homestead exemption did not yield the $415.6 million net tax base
assumed above, an adjustment was made in the assessment ratio.
The necessary ratio to yield the assumed net tax base was 0.385,
an amount well within two standard deviations of the mean assessment ratio for the city. This new assessment ratio was then applied
to all income/housing value groups, after which the $2,000 homestead
exemption was deducted for each housing unit. We then aggregated
the net assessed values within each income class over all housing

value classes. (3) Since the resulting distribution of net assessed
housing values by income classes is based on the census definition
of income, we shifted the assessed values in the same manner
as described in Chapter 4. Essentially, therefore, we are assuming
that shifted income units took their assessed housing values with
them. This then results in a distribution of the residential property
tax base by income class for owner-occupiers.

For rental residences, a three-step method was required.
(1) From the gross rental value/income matrix we had to account
first for residents of public housing. Although they are assumed
not to pay property taxes, in Atlanta all public housing residents
in 1970 paid a minimum of $24 per month in rent and, therefore,
are included in the census tabulations. We, therefore, used the
results of a local survey of public housing residents[12] to allocate
public housing residents by rental class and income class. These
were then subtracted from the census table entries. (2) The net
counts in each cell were then multiplied by the appropriate rental
class mark and aggregated over all rental classes within an
income class. (3) The gross rental distribution was then shifted in
the same manner as for the owner-occupiers so that the income
distribution conformed to the one used throughout this study. From
the aggregate tax base, a constant average tax rate can be determined
as before, which would yield any desired level of residential
property tax revenues. This rate times the income-class residential
property tax base then yields estimates of taxes for each income
group.

General Income Tax Base
by Income Class

Determination of the burden of two types of income taxes
required computing, from the reconstructed distribution of income,
the expected amount of taxable income, and income tax paid for
each income class while taking into account the distribution of
family size. We began by adjusting our broad-based income distribution to include only those income sources that are taxable under
Georgia law. The resulting "adjusted gross income" was found
by subtracting nontaxable income sources and adjusting for underreporting of taxable incomes. Nontaxable income sources used in
our broad-based definition of income include imputed rental incomes,
nonwage labor incomes, transfer incomes, and one-half of the
capital gains incomes (since it was assumed that all of the reported
net capital gains were in the form of long-term capital gains).
Our income distribution corrected for underreporting of incomes to
the census; however, comparison of total income by incomes
source—for example, wages and salaries—with those reported to

the IRS[13] indicate that these sources are also underreported to the
IRS. We therefore, adjusted our income estimates for the city
using the ratio of Atlanta SMSA income reported on federal income
tax returns relative to our income amounts for each of the three
income sources—wages and salaries, proprietorship income, and
property income. The respective ratios are 0.922, 0.608, and
0.722 and are assumed to be the same for each income class.
This adjustment results in a matrix of AGI by income class and
family size.

From adjusted gross income by income class and family size,
we subtracted the amount of exemptions allowed each family
($1,500 for an individual; $3,000 for man and wife, and $600 per
additional dependent). The level of deductions attributable to
each income class had to be estimated indirectly from data published
by the state. These data reveal total adjusted gross income (AGI)
and net taxable income (NTI) accruing from each of 21 AGI income
classes. Since NTI is derived from AGI by subtracting exemptions
and deductions, we computed an estimate of the amount of exemptions attributable to each AGI income class using average family
sizes by income class. We then assumed that the remainder of
the difference between AGI and NTI was due to deductions and,
for each AGI income class, determined the ratio of estimated
deductions to total AGI within the class. It was assumed that
these deduction ratios were constant across all family sizes within
an income class.

Subtracting estimated deductions and exemptions from AGI in
each of the income-class/family-size cells yielded a matrix of
estimated NTI by income class and family size as shown in Table 5.3.
The existing state income tax rate structure was then applied to
this matrix to yield estimates of total state income tax levied on
residents of Atlanta in 1970. The aggregate value of estimated
taxes paid using the methods described here is $33,124,455.

The estimated amount appears to be an overestimate of the
actual Georgia income tax liability assumed by Atlantans in 1970.
The actual tax yield from all of Fulton County was slightly greater
than $36 million, and, as was shown in Table 3.1, using state
revenue department data we estimated that the amount of state
tax liability for Atlanta was $26.8 million. This implies that either
the method outlined in this chapter is in error or that Atlantans
grossly underreport incomes. At least some underreporting is
likely, for when AGI, as reported to the IRS from the Atlanta SMSA,
is compared with the amount reported to the State of Georgia, it
was found that state AGI is only 88 percent of that reported to the
federal government.

There were thus two alternatives open to us given the discrepancy
in results. We could have adjusted downward all AGI entries by a
constant proportion such that the adjusted sum just equaled $26.8

TABLE 5.3

Estimated Net Taxable Income
by Income Class and Family Size
(dollars)

Income Class	Family Size					
	1	2	3	4	5	6
0-1	0	0	0	0	0	0
1-2	0	0	0	0	0	0
2-3	0	0	0	0	0	0
3-4	0	0	0	0	0	0
4-5	503	0	0	0	0	0
5-6	1,468	0	0	0	0	0
6-7	2,444	0	0	0	0	0
7-8	3,410	606	0	0	0	0
8-9	4,197	1,585	985	385	0	0
9-10	4,898	2,472	1,872	1,272	672	0
10-12	5,866	3,496	2,896	2,296	1,696	496
12-15	7,554	5,358	4,758	4,158	3,558	2,358
15-25	10,252	8,471	7,871	7,271	6,671	5,471
>25	23,554	20,247	19,647	19,047	18,447	17,247

Source: Compiled by the authors.

million. However, since this amount, too, was an estimate, we
decided to determine the income tax burdens and incidence on the
basis of the larger AGI base, keeping in mind that the results
reflect a likely upper limit on tax burdens by income class.

Consumption Base by Income Class

In determining the burden of tax-induced changes in the prices
of goods and services, excluding housing, we encountered some
rather severe data deficiencies. Since consumption by both
family size and income class was required, it was necessary to
utilize findings from surveys of consumer expenditures. Unfortunately, no adequate data source was found that focuses on the population
under investigation.

We first considered using the IRS table of sales taxes for
deduction purposes in the federal income tax. Unfortunately,
these data neglect sales taxes paid on major consumer durables;
therefore, when used to estimate total sales taxable consumption

by Atlantans, the estimated level of consumption is only slightly
over $600 million rather than the $1,249.08 million estimated in
Chapter 3 above. Further, the IRS data exclude consumption of
non-sales-taxable services. Thus, we turned to alternative data
sources.

The data source used was the Bureau of Labor Statistics' (BLS)
1960-61 Survey of Consumer Expenditures.[14] We acknowledge that
there are severe problems with these data. The income concept
used does not match ours, and the date of the survey (1960 and
1961) suggests that, because relative prices and perhaps tastes
have since changed, a different composition of expenditures now
holds. (The BLS is currently undertaking another survey of consumer
expenditures, but unfortunately the results are not yet available.)
Further, since it was necessary to use a cross-tabulation of income
by family size, some cells of the sample contain relatively few
observations; therefore, particular families' circumstances may
produce rather unlikely results. This is especially true for the
lowest income class ($0-1,000). For example, families of five
in urban areas with income of less than $1,000 are shown to have
average total consumption expenditures of $6,333 and average
number of years of education of 15 for the head of the family.

The following procedure was used to determine from these
data the burden by income class of tax-induced price changes.
We first determined from the information on U.S. urban families
the percent of before-tax family income (census income concept)
for each family size (1-6) and income class that was current
consumption, excluding payment for shelter. Second, we determined
a cumulative distribution of before-tax income over the 10 income
classes provided by the BLS. We also determined the cumulative
distribution of incomes in our estimated Atlanta income distribution
over the 14 income classes. We then assumed that the proportion
of income spent would be approximately the same for families
in the two income distributions who were situated in the same
relative positions within the cumulative income distributions.
Thus, for example, the median of our income distribution falls
within the $15,000-$25,000 income class whereas the BLS median
occurred in the $6,000-$7,500 income class. Therefore, the
proportions of income consumed by different family sizes were
assumed to be approximately equal in these two income classes.
When this new matrix of average propensities to consume by family
size was applied to the money income levels in each income class
(excluding imputed rental income and nonwage labor income), a
matrix of consumption levels by family size and income was derived,
which, for all but the two lowest income classes, appeared a priori
reasonable. We then arbitrarily adjusted the levels in the lowest
two income classes such that consumption was a monotonically
increasing function of income and family size. It was this

consumption matrix (shown in Table 5.4) that was then employed
to determine burdens of the tax-induced price changes.

TABLE 5.4

Assumed Consumption
by Income Class and Family Size*
(in dollars)

Income Class	1	2	3	4	5	6
0-1	1,200	1,250	1,300	1,400	1,475	1,550
1-2	1,500	1,600	1,650	1,700	1,750	1,850
2-3	1,700	1,900	1,940	1,990	1,995	2,135
3-4	2,510	2,610	2,750	3,180	3,260	3,620
4-5	2,930	3,320	3,480	3,980	4,330	5,040
5-6	3,480	4,030	4,330	4,770	5,130	5,800
6-7	3,960	4,730	5,180	5,350	5,820	6,420
7-8	4,430	5,260	5,610	5,930	6,310	6,660
8-9	4,850	5,600	6,120	6,570	6,780	6,850
9-10	5,280	6,130	6,660	7,100	7,150	7,460
10-12	5,894	6,650	7,450	7,870	7,740	8,430
12-15	6,290	7,740	8,590	8,990	9,260	9,430
15-25	7,370	10,000	11,000	11,400	12,100	13,100
>25	18,900	20,970	23,950	25,270	26,580	27,240

*Excluding housing expenditures

Source: Compiled by the authors.

The major use of the consumption matrix was for computation
of the burden of the general sales tax falling on consumers. For
this tax, the consumption matrix was adjusted in an attempt to
exclude items not taxable under the general sales tax—for example,
services of physicians. Unfortunately, the source of data precludes
any easy and accurate adjustment. The method used was analogous
to that above for total consumption, except that instead of using
all current consumption we limited ourselves to the following
list of consumer items: food, tobacco, alcoholic beverages, house
furnishings and equipment, clothing, personal care, medical care,
reading, automobile transportation, and other expenditures. This
excluded expenditures on fuel, light, refrigeration and water,
household operations, recreation, and education. The resulting

matrix is admittedly arbitrary. Further, the estimated total taxable
consumption of $1 billion is somewhat smaller than the $1.2
billion estimated in Chapter 3 above.

Wage and Salary Tax Base
by Income Class

To estimate tax burdens by income class for the portion of
any tax passed backwards to labor inputs, we used as the base
the wage and salary income of our constructed income distribution.
Aggregating overall income classes yields a total local base of
$1.3 billion. This amount, of course, accounts for underreporting
of wage and salary incomes. We assumed that, because it may
be more difficult to avoid a payroll tax through underreporting,
this entire base would be subject to the tax.

METHOD OF COMPUTING
FEDERAL TAX OFFSETS

To calculate net tax burdens it is necessary to deduct the
decrease in federal tax liability for taxpayers who itemize deductions.
Federal tax laws provide for deduction of all direct taxes (by direct
we mean taxes levied directly on the taxpaying unit, not taxes they
"pay" through forward or backward shifting) paid to state and local
governments.* The method employed for estimating the value
of such offsets was as follows.

From IRS data[15] we determined, for (1) joint returns and (2)
separate returns and returns of single persons (called "unrelated
individual returns," throughout this discussion), the proportion
of returns with itemized deductions within each adjusted gross
income class. Further, for these two types of returns we determined
the average marginal tax rates for each AGI class. This has the
advantage of weighting income classes by national family sizes
and thus alleviates the need to calculate the offsets by family size.

----

*The state of Georgia also provides for offsets on local taxes;
however, since the highest marginal rate in the state income tax is
only 6 percent (and this on net taxable incomes greater than $10,000),
we ignored the state tax in our analysis. Further, since Fulton
County accounts for almost one-fifth of the adjusted gross income
reported in the state of Georgia, the assumption that there would be
no secondary effects of the offsets would be a very strong assumption.

We assumed that, except for the residential property tax, Atlanta taxpayers in each AGI class itemized deductions in the same proportion as did taxpayers nationally. The estimated rates of itemization and marginal taxes are shown in Table 5.5.

TABLE 5.5

Federal Tax: Proportion Itemizing
and Marginal Rates

	Joint Returns		Single and Separate Returns	
	(1)	(2)	(3)	(4)
AGI Class	Proportion Itemizing	Effective Marginal Rates	Proportion Itemizing	Effective Marginal Rates
0-1	0.046	0	0.011	0.013
1-2	0.106	0.003	0.097	0.062
2-3	0.227	0.029	0.197	0.136
3-4	0.397	0.078	0.250	0.166
4-5	0.431	0.109	0.289	0.181
5-6	0.518	0.133	0.313	0.195
6-7	0.534	0.146	0.334	0.211
7-8	0.595	0.158	0.358	0.215
8-9	0.637	0.162	0.398	0.218
9-10	0.667	0.175	0.402	0.228
10-15	0.757	0.189	0.512	0.262
15-20	0.879	0.209	0.689	0.289
20-25	0.923	0.231	0.802	0.372
25-30	0.942	0.259	0.848	0.389
20-50	0.964	0.320	0.915	0.389
>50	0.981	0.447	0.948	0.487

Source: Compiled by the authors.

Upon determination of AGI within each of our family income classes, we multiplied the computed effective marginal tax rate times the proportion of family units assumed to itemize. This product, in turn, was multiplied by the direct local tax liability to obtain an estimate of the federal offset realized in each family income class. The same method was applied to unrelated individuals except that they were assumed to file as did single persons and separate return filers nationally. Thus, for example, if our income class $6,000-$7,000 is shown to have a mean AGI of $3,600 and

39.7 percent of the national filers in the $3,000-$4,000 AGI class itemize deductions and the mean marginal tax rate is 7.8 percent, then we assumed that 0.397 times 0.078 times any local tax estimated to be paid directly by representative taxpayers in our income class $6,000-$7,000 is offset by decreased federal tax liabilities.

A slightly different approach was used to estimate offsets for local residential property taxes. We assumed that, other things being equal, homeowners are more likely to itemize deductions than are renters, especially because of the mortgage interest offset provision of the federal income tax. From the percentages in columns (1) and (3) of Table 5.5 we determined the upper limit of unrelated individuals and families who could itemize. If the number of homeowners in an AGI group was greater than this upper limit, only the upper limit of owners was assumed to itemize and thus take advantage of the offset (unrelated individuals and families were handled separately in this determination). If the upper limit of itemizers was greater than the number of owners within an AGI class (as was true for the higher-income classes), all owners were assumed to take advantage of the federal offsets.

INCIDENCE RESULTS

As was noted in Chapter 3, in order to make meaningful comparisons of the burdens and incidence of the several taxes, we have assumed equal total yields from each tax. In our findings the burden of the tax by income class is reported in two ways. We present dollar estimates of taxes that "representative taxpaying units" within each income class would pay under the assumptions specified previously. In addition, for each of the taxes considered, we determined the proportion of total income accruing to each income class paid in the form of local taxes. These two measures of tax burden make possible comparisons both across income classes for a single tax and across taxes for varied income classes.

To measure the incidence of the tax, we employ a single statistic, the Gini ratio, which is used to describe the level of income equality or inequality observed within a population.* The aggregate pretax income distribution as constructed in Chapter 4

---

*The Gini concentration ratio (called the Gini ratio or Gini coefficient throughout the remainder of this monograph) varies from zero (the case of perfect equality) to one (the case of perfect inequality). We acknowledge that alternative single parameter indexes of equality are feasible (for example, the variance of the natural logarithm of income) and can lead to different conclusions about the relative levels of equality in a population.

is presented in Table 5.6. For purposes of comparison, the
Gini ratio associated with this distribution is 0.4668. Thus, any
Gini coefficient greater than this amount indicates an increase in
the concentration of income distribution due to the tax, and a
coefficient less than 0.4668 indicates that the tax would decrease
income inequality.

TABLE 5.6

Final Income Distribution

	Families		Unrelated Individuals		
	(1)	(2)	(3)	(4)	(5)
Income Class	Number	Percent of Total	Number	Percent of Total	Class Mean Income (dollars)
0-1	3,297	2.76	14,982	21.74	127
1-2	1,066	0.89	3,941	5.72	1,669
2-3	2,441	2.04	8,944	12.98	2,552
3-4	4,294	3.80	4,941	7.17	3,541
4-5	4,649	3.90	6,016	8.73	4,469
5-6	6,191	5.19	5,467	7.93	5,452
6-7	7,549	6.33	5,140	7.46	6,448
7-8	8,354	7.00	4,667	6.77	7,446
8-9	7,607	6.38	3,195	4.64	8,470
9-10	6,713	5.63	2,395	3.48	9,528
10-12	13,649	11.44	3,228	4.68	10,953
12-15	15,406	12.91	2,474	3.59	13,394
15-25	25,827	21.65	2,154	3.12	18,692
>25	12,248	10.27	1,376	2.00	42,601
Total	119,291	100.00	68,920	100.00	—

Source: Compiled by the authors.

To aid in the understanding of the overall income distributional
effects of the several taxes, the above measures of burden and
incidence are presented, when applicable, for both the income
sources and the income uses sides. In addition, we provide
numerical estimates of how the original statutory burden of the
tax is altered due to the federal income tax offset. Finally, we

report the total net effect on the distribution of income of each
of the local taxes under consideration.

Estimated Burden and Incidence
of the Property Tax

In Chapter 3, it was determined that 36.4 percent of the total
local property tax base in Atlanta was residential housing, either
owner-occupied or rental. Thus, we assumed that 36.4 percent,
or $7.28 million, of the total tax yield of $20 million is derived
from residential housing.

In the first section of the present chapter, we outlined two
alternative ways of estimating the residential property tax base
by income class. From such estimates and the required total yield
of $7.28 million, we derive two alternative estimates of the gross
burden by income class of the residential portion of the property
tax. Columns (1) and (2) of Table 5.7 show the resulting burdens
in terms of required taxes per income-receiving unit and the
proportion of class income that would necessarily be paid by
income class under the assumptions that the income elasticity of
demand for housing is 0.75 for owners and 0.5 for renters.
The first two columns of Table 5.8 show the analogous estimates
derived using the income/housing-value estimates reported in the
census. Below these burden estimates are the net-of-tax Gini
coefficients.

The results shown in the first set of columns of Tables 5.7
and 5.8 indicate the sensitivity of the conclusions to estimation
methods used. While the distribution of incomes net of taxes
under the assumption of constant elasticity of demand suggest
that the property tax decreases income inequality very slightly
or at least does not increase inequality, the estimates using the
cross-tabulated data suggest that the property tax results in greater
inequality of incomes.

Further information regarding the sensitivity of the conclusions
to the assumptions regarding the income elasticity of demand
for housing can be observed from the following set of results
obtained when the incidence of the residential property tax was
estimated using three alternative sets of elasticity assumptions.

Income Elasticity	Gini Coefficient
1.1 for owners; 0.9 for renters	0.4664
0.65 for owners; 0.5 for renters	0.4668
0.5 for owners; 0.5 for renters	0.4670

Thus, when the first set of estimates (those most similar to those
found by deLeeuw), is used, the property tax is somewhat progressive

TABLE 5.7

Estimated Burdens and Incidence of Property Tax
under Constant Elasticity Assumption

Income Class	Before Offset		After Offset		Uses Side		Total Net Burden	
	(1) Tax/ Unit*	(2) Tax/ Income	(3) Tax/ Unit	(4) Tax/ Income	(5) Tax/ Unit	(6) Tax/ Income	(7) Tax/ Unit	(8) Tax/ Income
0–1	2.13	0.0167	2.13	0.0167	3.85	0.0303	5.98	0.0470
1–2	7.61	0.0046	7.61	0.0046	4.83	0.0029	12.44	0.0075
2–3	8.85	0.0035	8.81	0.0035	5.51	0.0022	14.32	0.0057
3–4	10.08	0.0028	10.05	0.0028	8.38	0.0024	18.43	0.0052
4–5	14.46	0.0032	14.24	0.0032	10.26	0.0023	24.50	0.0055
5–6	17.37	0.0032	16.97	0.0031	12.64	0.0023	29.61	0.0054
6–7	20.64	0.0032	19.95	0.0031	14.83	0.0023	34.78	0.0054
7–8	25.43	0.0034	24.14	0.0032	16.56	0.0022	40.70	0.0054
8–9	29.41	0.0035	27.89	0.0033	18.10	0.0021	45.99	0.0054
9–10	32.71	0.0034	30.80	0.0032	19.84	0.0021	50.64	0.0053
10–12	37.50	0.0034	34.93	0.0032	22.34	0.0020	57.27	0.0052
12–15	46.97	0.0035	42.41	0.0032	25.91	0.0019	68.32	0.0051
15–25	68.22	0.0036	60.22	0.0032	34.29	0.0018	94.51	0.0050
>25	151.32	0.0035	114.16	0.0027	73.97	0.0017	188.13	0.0044

Gini Coefficient 0.4667   0.4668   0.4669   0.4670

*Tax/Units in dollars

Source: Compiled by the authors.

84

TABLE 5.8

Estimated Burdens and Incidence of Property Tax
Using Census Data

Income Class	Before Offset		After Offset		Uses Side		Total Net Burden	
	(1) Tax/Unit*	(2) Tax/Income	(3) Tax/Unit	(4) Tax/Income	(5) Tax/Unit	(6) Tax/Income	(7) Tax/Unit	(8) Tax/Income
0–1	14.79	0.1156	14.79	0.1156	3.85	0.0303	18.64	0.1459
1–2	14.95	0.0089	14.95	0.0089	4.83	0.0029	19.78	0.0118
2–3	15.06	0.0059	14.99	0.0059	5.51	0.0022	20.50	0.0081
3–4	18.06	0.0050	18.00	0.0050	8.38	0.0024	26.38	0.0074
4–5	20.38	0.0046	20.07	0.0045	10.26	0.0023	30.33	0.0068
5–6	21.95	0.0040	21.45	0.0039	12.64	0.0023	34.09	0.0062
6–7	23.77	0.0037	22.98	0.0036	14.83	0.0023	37.81	0.0059
7–8	30.24	0.0041	28.70	0.0038	16.56	0.0022	45.26	0.0060
8–9	30.42	0.0036	28.85	0.0034	18.10	0.0021	46.95	0.0055
9–10	30.24	0.0032	28.47	0.0030	19.84	0.0021	48.31	0.0051
10–12	39.63	0.0036	36.91	0.0034	22.34	0.0020	59.25	0.0054
12–15	39.57	0.0030	35.73	0.0027	25.91	0.0019	61.64	0.0046
15–25	60.07	0.0032	53.03	0.0028	34.29	0.0018	87.32	0.0046
>25	129.69	0.0030	97.84	0.0023	73.97	0.0017	171.81	0.0040

Gini Coefficient 0.4671   0.4672   0.4669   0.4674

*Tax/Units in dollars.

Source: Compiled by the authors.

85

if lowering of the Gini coefficient is used as an indicator of
progressivity. At the other extreme, using 0.5 as the estimates
of income elasticity yields results that indicate the property tax
is regressive. It is therefore obvious that the incidence of the
residential property tax hinges upon the "correct" income elasticity
of demand for housing.

Of equal interest to this sensitivity of the incidence of the tax
to income elasticities is the observed differences in results reported
in Tables 5.7 and 5.8. As indicated earlier in this chapter, the
census tabulation of housing values and incomes, when employed
in a weighted least-squares analysis, yielded elasticity estimates
that did not differ significantly from 1.0. The results shown in
Table 5.7 were based on the fairly conservative assumption of an
elasticity of only 0.75, and the residential property tax still was
found to lower income inequality. Yet the same census data, when
used directly, indicates the tax increases income inequality. One
possible explanation for this divergence in findings is that income
elasticities are not constant over all income levels, as is assumed
in regression analyses. The assumption is especially likely to be
less than ideal for the lowest and highest levels of income.
Of course, the regression analyses reported upon above certainly
do not explain all variations in housing demand, even when they
include other explanatory variables. For example, Carliner,[16]
with his individual-level panel data, reports coefficients of determination of slightly greater than 0.3, implying that nearly 70
percent of the variations in the dependent variable (real housing
value) is left unexplained even when five variables in addition to
income are included in the analysis. Although R^2 statistics are
not crucial to the legitimacy of empirical analyses, using the
results to further predict actual relations may lead to questionable
conclusions. On the other hand, although we have attempted to
adjust the income data to correspond more closely to normal or
permanent income, to the extent that such corrections were incorrect
or incomplete, there may still be numerous "low-income families"
in our distribution who, in fact, have substantially larger normal
incomes and therefore are among the numerous low-income families
with housing values greater than $40,000. Finally, of course,
one may conclude that, except for the lowest income class (about
which we probably know very little anyway), the differences in
the numbers in columns (2) of Tables 5.7 and 5.8 are not substantial
enough to negate the general conclusion that the residential property
tax, before federal tax offset, is very close to proportional.

The owner-occupied portion of the residential property tax
is assumed to be partially offset by decreased federal tax liability.
Using the methods outlined above, burden estimates net of federal
offsets taken by homeowners are presented in columns (3) and (4)
of Tables 5.7 and 5.8. These offsets increase income inequality
due to the progressive federal tax rates.

In Chapter 3 we found that 14.1 percent of the total property tax yield* was in the form of nonexported price increases. Thus, we assumed that $2.83 million of the $20 million tax yield would be indirectly borne by local residents in the form of general price increases. Using the methods shown in the section "Methods of Computing Tax Bases by Income Class," above, the net burdens of the property tax on the uses side were computed with the results shown in columns (5) and (6) of Tables 5.7 and 5.8. These burdens, being slightly regressive, tend to increase income inequality, as shown by the Gini coefficient.

The total net burdens on Atlanta residents of a property tax that yields $20 million are shown in the final columns of Tables 5.7 and 5.8. Under the constant elasticity assumption, the tax is observed to be only very slightly regressive when both burdens on residential housing and income-uses side are considered along with federal tax offsets. On the other hand, the Gini coefficient estimated using the income/housing value approach to the question of property tax incidence suggests that the tax is regressive since both the federal tax offsets and burden on the uses side contribute to further regressivity. Unfortunately, therefore, one can conclude only that the property tax is likely to be either very slightly or quite regressive depending upon the underlying assumptions regarding the income/housing value relationship.

Estimated Burden and Incidence
of the Payroll Tax

In Chapter 3, it was found that the total payroll tax base was $2,473.59 million so that a tax rate of 0.81 percent is required to yield the desired $20 million. It was also found that the tax burden on the sources side on Atlanta residents was $777.12 T_L (million). When T_L = 0.81 percent the actual tax burden on the sources side on Atlanta residents is $6.29 million. Using the methods outlined above, the burden, by income class, of the $6.29 million was computed with the results shown in columns (1) and (2) of Table 5.9. Also shown there is the Gini coefficient, which indicates that the burden on the sources side slightly decreases income inequality.

We base the federal tax offset on the payroll tax before any tax-induced changes in wages and salaries occur. Therefore, the tax offsets were computed based on a local payroll tax yield of $9.99 million. When these offsets by income class are deducted

---

*Recall that under our assumptions the tax yield equals the tax burden.

TABLE 5.9

Estimated Burdens and Incidence of Payroll Tax

Income Class	Sources Side				Uses Side		Total Net Burden	
	Before Offset		After Offset					
	(1) Tax/Unit*	(2) Tax/Income	(3) Tax/Unit	(4) Tax/Income	(5) Tax/Unit	(6) Tax/Income	(7) Tax/Unit	(8) Tax/Income
0-1	0.09	0.0007	0.09	0.0007	1.71	0.0134	1.80	0.0141
1-2	2.10	0.0012	2.10	0.0012	2.14	0.0013	4.24	0.0025
2-3	3.39	0.0013	3.37	0.0013	2.44	0.0010	5.81	0.0023
3-4	4.34	0.0012	4.32	0.0012	3.71	0.0010	8.03	0.0022
4-5	7.16	0.0016	6.99	0.0016	4.55	0.0010	11.54	0.0026
5-6	10.77	0.0020	10.38	0.0019	5.60	0.0010	15.98	0.0029
6-7	15.68	0.0024	14.69	0.0023	6.57	0.0010	21.26	0.0033
7-8	21.55	0.0029	19.77	0.0026	7.34	0.0010	27.11	0.0036
8-9	27.02	0.0032	24.04	0.0028	8.02	0.0009	32.06	0.0037
9-10	31.89	0.0033	27.95	0.0029	8.79	0.0009	36.74	0.0038
10-12	38.31	0.0035	32.22	0.0029	9.90	0.0009	42.12	0.0038
12-15	48.83	0.0036	37.82	0.0028	11.48	0.0008	49.30	0.0036
15-25	67.20	0.0036	51.99	0.0028	15.20	0.0008	67.19	0.0036
>25	112.45	0.0026	56.45	0.0013	32.79	0.0008	89.24	0.0021

Gini Coefficient 0.4667   0.4668   0.4668   0.4668

*Tax/Units in dollars.

Source: Compiled by the authors.

from columns (1) and (2) of Table 5.9, we obtain the results shown
in columns (3) and (4) of that table. Once again the effect of
the offset is to decrease the progressivity of the payroll tax.

The resulting increases in prices paid by Atlanta residents of
$223.48 T_L million imply that, with the required payroll tax rate of
0.81 percent, Atlanta residents will bear $1.81 million in tax
burdens on the income uses side. The burdens by income class
were then determined as outlined above. The results, which
indicate the basic proportional characteristic of the uses side of
the tax, are shown in columns (5) and (6) of Table 5.9.

Finally, the aggregate net burden and incidence of local payroll
tax, which yields $20 million, is shown in columns (7) and (8) of
Table 5.9. We conclude from these findings that, in general, the
tax is approximately proportional, with the only major regressivity
occurring in the lowest income class.

Estimated Burden and Incidence
of the General Sales Tax

In Chapter 3, it was shown that a general sales tax imposed
burdens on both the income uses and sources side. It was determined
there that on the income uses side, there are two partially offsetting
effects. On the one hand, there is the increased prices of taxable
goods due to the sales tax itself. For Atlanta residents, the increases
in prices due to the $20 million tax yield were found to be $9.28
million. On the other hand, the decrease in prices of all goods
produced in Sectors X and Y due to the decrease in the price of labor
were found to equal $2.22 million (since dP_x x_A was –$250.05 T_x
million and dP_y y_A was –$48.64 T_x million, and the necessary
tax rate to yield $20 million was 0.743 percent). To ascertain the
burden on the uses side of the sales tax, we thus first estimated
the burden of the increased prices due to the tax itself (applied
to the sales taxable consumption matrix) and deducted from it the
burden of the decreased prices (applied to the total consumption
matrix). The net results are shown in columns (1) and (2) of
Table 5.10 and indicate the general regressivity of the burden on
the uses side.

As in the case of the payroll tax, the federal tax offset was
applied to the increase in prices due to the tax before any tax-induced
price decrease. Thus, the federal tax offset was applied to the
$9.28 million tax yield. When these offsets are netted from the
results shown in columns (1) and (2), we obtain the burdens shown
in columns (3) and (4) of Table 5.10. Once again the offset
increases the regressivity of the local tax.

For the decreased wages—that is, the burden on the income
sources side—we used the wage and salary base methodology

TABLE 5.10

Estimated Burdens and Incidence of General Sales Tax

Income Class	Uses Side — Before Offset		Uses Side — After Offset		Sources Side		Total Net Burden	
	(1) Tax/Unit*	(2) Tax/Income	(3) Tax/Unit	(4) Tax/Income	(5) Tax/Unit	(6) Tax/Income	(7) Tax/Unit	(8) Tax/Income
0-1	7.44	0.0585	7.44	0.0585	0.05	0.0004	7.49	0.0589
1-2	7.50	0.0045	7.50	0.0045	1.14	0.0007	8.64	0.0052
2-3	7.76	0.0031	7.71	0.0030	1.85	0.0007	9.56	0.0037
3-4	12.73	0.0036	12.67	0.0036	2.37	0.0007	15.04	0.0043
4-5	16.28	0.0036	15.95	0.0036	3.90	0.0009	19.85	0.0045
5-6	20.65	0.0038	20.02	0.0037	5.87	0.0011	25.89	0.0048
6-7	28.31	0.0044	26.87	0.0042	8.54	0.0013	35.41	0.0055
7-8	31.94	0.0043	29.81	0.0040	11.74	0.0016	41.55	0.0056
8-9	34.20	0.0040	31.14	0.0037	14.72	0.0017	45.86	0.0054
9-10	35.68	0.0038	32.07	0.0034	17.38	0.0018	49.45	0.0052
10-12	38.74	0.0035	33.65	0.0031	20.88	0.0019	54.53	0.0050
12-15	44.64	0.0033	36.31	0.0027	26.61	0.0020	62.92	0.0047
15-25	59.52	0.0032	48.39	0.0026	36.62	0.0020	85.01	0.0046
>25	123.28	0.0029	72.05	0.0017	61.28	0.0014	133.33	0.0031
Gini Coefficient	0.4670		0.4672		0.4667		0.4671	

*Tax/Units in dollars.

Source: Compiled by the authors.

outlined above with the total decrease in Atlanta income sources estimated to be $3.42 million for the $20 million sales tax. The burdens on the sources side are given in columns (5) and (6) of Table 5.10.

The net total burden and incidence of the local sales tax are shown in columns (7) and (8) of Table 5.10. It is apparent from this table that the incidence of the local sales tax is such as to decrease income equality in the locality.

Estimated Burden and Incidence
of the Income Taxes

As was implied in Chapter 3, the entire burden of the income taxes under investigation (the surtax and add-on) falls on the income sources side. Thus, the only part of the tax burden not paid by Atlanta residents is the federal tax liability offset. Table 5.11 contains the results before and after federal offsets for both types of income taxes. Since the Georgia state income tax is mildly progressive (with marginal rates ranging from 1 percent to 6 percent), the burdens shown in Table 5.11 are also progressive. The surtax is, of course, somewhat more progressive than the add-on tax with the federal offset decreasing the progressivity in both cases.

SUMMARY

In this chapter we have utilized the findings of the previous chapters to estimate empirically both the burdens by income class and the incidence of the four equal-yield taxes under investigation. We first outlined the estimation methods used in determining alternative tax bases by income class. After explaining the method used to estimate federal income tax offsets for local tax burdens, we reported the results of the burden and incidence estimates. All results were given regarding the tax burden on both the income sources and income uses sides. When both sides were accounted for and federal offsets were netted out, the results indicate that either form of income tax is most progressive while the sales tax is most regressive. Our results further indicate that the payroll tax, as defined here, is essentially proportional while the property tax is either slightly regressive or slightly progressive, depending on the estimation method used and the assumptions made. The following chapter contains a more direct comparison of net burdens by income class across these various taxes.

TABLE 5.11

Estimated Burdens and Incidence of Two Types of Income Tax

Income Class	Add-on Rate				Surtax			
	Before Offset		After Offset		Before Offset		After Offset	
	(1) Tax/ Unit*	(2) Tax/ Income	(3) Tax/ Unit	(4) Tax/ Income	(5) Tax/ Unit	(6) Tax/ Income	(7) Tax/ Unit	(8) Tax/ Income
0-1	0	0	0	0	0	0	0	0
1-2	0	0	0	0	0	0	0	0
2-3	0	0	0	0	0	0	0	0
3-4	0	0	0	0	0	0	0	0
4-5	4.65	0.0010	4.50	0.0010	1.32	0.0003	1.29	0.0003
5-6	16.53	0.0030	16.15	0.0030	6.21	0.0011	6.06	0.0011
6-7	30.82	0.0048	29.60	0.0046	13.96	0.0022	13.40	0.0021
7-8	48.27	0.0065	45.75	0.0061	24.67	0.0033	23.38	0.0031
8-9	68.35	0.0081	63.81	0.0075	38.58	0.0046	35.90	0.0042
9-10	85.65	0.0090	78.99	0.0083	51.47	0.0054	47.46	0.0050
10-12	110.92	0.0101	99.82	0.0091	75.65	0.0069	68.07	0.0062
12-15	150.79	0.0112	129.40	0.0097	121.05	0.0090	103.88	0.0078
15-25	212.75	0.0114	182.45	0.0098	207.88	0.0111	178.23	0.0095
>25	490.12	0.0115	336.58	0.0079	680.54	0.0159	467.34	0.0109
Gini Coefficient	0.4654		0.4660		0.4645		0.4652	

*Tax/Units in dollars.

Source: Compiled by the authors.

NOTES

1. Interestingly, there were not substantial vertical inequities found in the assessment ratios by housing value class. This question was analyzed more fully in L. D. Schroeder, W. Sheftall, and D. L. Sjoquist, "Variations in Property Tax Assessment Ratios: The Case of Fulton County," Atlanta Economic Review (forthcoming).

2. Housing All Atlantans: Subsidy Programs (Atlanta: Atlanta Regional Metropolitan Planning Commission, 1970).

3. Frank deLeeuw, "The Demand for Housing: A Review of Cross-Section Evidence," Review of Economics and Statistics 53 (February 1971): 1.

4. Ibid., p. 10.

5. S. J. Maisel, J. B. Burnham, and J. S. Austin, "The Demand for Housing: A Comment," Review of Economics and Statistics 53 (November 1971): 410-13.

6. Ibid., p. 413.

7. Geoffrey Carliner, "Income Elasticity of Housing Demand," Review of Economics and Statistics 55 (November 1973): 528-32.

8. U. S. Bureau of the Census, Census of Housing: 1970. Metropolitan Housing Characteristics, Final Report HC(2)-15 (Washington, D. C.: Government Printing Office, 1972).

9. Ibid.

10. Ibid.

11. George E. Peterson, "The Regressivity of the Residential Property Tax," Urban Institute Working Paper S1207-10 (Washington: Urban Institute, 1972).

12. Housing All Atlantans: Subsidy Programs, op. cit.

13. Internal Revenue Service, Statistics of Income—1969, Individual Income Tax Returns (Washington, D. C.: Government Printing Office, 1972).

14. U. S. Department of Labor, Bureau of Labor Statistics, "Consumer Expenditures and Income Cross-Classification of Family Characteristics (Urban United States), 1960-1961," Survey of Consumer Expenditures, BLS-Report 237-38, Supplement 2-Part A (Washington, D. C.: Government Printing Office, 1964).

15. Internal Revenue Service, op. cit.

16. Carliner, op. cit.

6

SUMMARY

Criticism of the property tax has led local governments to consider other taxes as alternatives to the property tax. Two important issues relevant to the decision of which, if any, alternative tax should be employed are the extent of exporting and incidence of the various taxes. This study has addressed itself to these two issues.

We constructed a two-sector general-equilibrium model based upon previous work in the area of tax incidence. Using the theoretical implications of this model, we developed empirical estimates of the net tax burden on Atlanta residents and the incidence of these burdens by income class for the property tax, payroll tax, sales tax, and income tax.

The theoretical model presented in Chapter 2 is a two-sector general-equilibrium model in which the normal assumptions regarding demand, production, and factor payments were made. It was assumed, however, that the two sectors constitute only a small part of a larger economy. We then assumed that labor is mobile within the two sectors but not between the two sectors and the rest of the economy, while capital and products are perfectly mobile within the entire economy. A general equilibrium was assumed to be attained within the two sectors while only a partial equilibrium was attained within the whole economy.

Upon solving the model and inserting the assumed values of certain parameters, we obtained expressions for the burden on Atlanta residents of each of the taxes. These expressions, together with estimates of federal income tax offsets, were then used in Chapter 3 to estimate the percent of the tax burden for each tax that would be exported—that is, the percent of the burden that would fall upon persons outside Atlanta. The results of these estimates are as follows:

Local Tax	Percent of Total Tax Yield Exported
Property	47.8
Payroll	67.6
General sales	50.3
Income surtax	21.3
Income add-on	18.4

The implications of these results are obvious. Substitution of a payroll tax for the property tax will result in a significant decrease in the amount of taxes Atlanta residents ultimately pay, while adoption of a sales tax will decrease only slightly the total net local burden. On the other hand, use of either type of income tax as a replacement for the property tax will increase significantly the burden on Atlanta residents.

In addition to these net burdens of alternative taxes, the incidence of the burden across income classes is also of importance in the policy decision. To estimate the income distributional effects of the alternative taxes, a local distribution of income was first constructed, with an outline of the income construction process given in Chapter 4. As explained there, the resultant distribution reflects a broad-based definition of income including income categories excluded from the census definition of income and accounting for underreporting of income to the census. In addition, the final distribution includes a disaggregation of income by income type and family size, thus making possible more accurate estimates of tax bases by income class.

In Chapter 5, the results of Chapter 3 and 4 were combined to derive estimates of tax yields by income class for each of the alternative equal-yield taxes. To facilitate comparison of these findings, Table 6.1 is presented, which shows, for each tax, the final net (after federal income tax offset) tax yield as a proportion of pretax incomes for the 14 income classes used in this study. In addition, the lower panel of the table shows the final Gini coefficient, local tax yields on both the income sources and uses sides, and finally the total net tax burden after all exporting (including federal tax offsets).

As shown by the Gini coefficients, the results suggest that the sales tax would tend to increase income inequality while the payroll tax would have little effect on income distribution. On the other hand, the property tax is shown to be very slightly progressive, and the income tax, with the lowest income classes experiencing no burdens, is shown allowing for the greatest decrease in income inequality.

TABLE 6.1

Final Estimated Burdens and Incidence
of Alternative Taxes

Income Class	Tax/Income				
	Property Tax	Payroll Tax	Sales Tax	Income Tax Add-On	Income Surtax
0-1	0.0338	0.0141	0.0589	0	0
1-2	0.0056	0.0025	0.0052	0	0
2-3	0.0045	0.0023	0.0037	0	0
3-4	0.0041	0.0022	0.0043	0	0
4-5	0.0043	0.0026	0.0045	0.0010	0.0003
5-6	0.0045	0.0029	0.0048	0.0030	0.0011
6-7	0.0047	0.0033	0.0055	0.0046	0.0021
7-8	0.0049	0.0036	0.0056	0.0061	0.0031
8-9	0.0049	0.0037	0.0054	0.0075	0.0042
9-10	0.0050	0.0038	0.0052	0.0083	0.0050
10-12	0.0049	0.0038	0.0050	0.0091	0.0062
12-15	0.0049	0.0036	0.0047	0.0097	0.0078
15-25	0.0050	0.0036	0.0046	0.0098	0.0095
>25	0.0051	0.0021	0.0031	0.0079	0.0109
Gini	0.4667	0.4668	0.4671	0.4660	0.4652
Local Burdens					
Uses	$11.36	$1.81 m	$7.06 m	—	—
Sources	—	6.29	3.42	$20.0 m	$20.0 m
Net of Offsets	10.32	6.48	9.94	16.32	15.74

Source: Compiled by the authors.

IMPLICATIONS OF THE RESULTS

Directly apparent from these empirical results is the trade-off
between minimizing local net tax burdens and increasing the
equality of the income distribution. Although local income taxes
are the most progressive of the taxes considered, they also result
in the largest local burden, since the only form of tax exporting
for income taxes is via the federal tax offset. On the other hand,
the regressive sales and proportional payroll taxes allow for
the greatest amount of tax exporting. In a sense then, the current
and much maligned property tax may involve a compromise, being

almost proportional but permitting one-half of the burden to be exported.

These implications have, of course, been drawn from a single case study of one major central city. Although it is not possible to extrapolate these empirical findings exactly to all other central cities, it is reasonable to consider how the results of the current case study might relate to other cities of comparable size. Without repeating the calculations for other cities, it is not possible to make precise statements regarding the exporting of local taxes from other central cities. However, by making comparisons of socioeconomic, financial, and industrial characteristics between Atlanta and other central cities of similar populations, it is possible to obtain an idea of the applicability of our results to other cities. On the other hand, our estimates of the incidence across income classes will be closely approximated in other cities. Thus, we focus primarily on tax exporting.

Tables 6.2 and 6.3 show certain demographic and financial attributes of 20 cities ranging in population from 310,000 to 1,233,000. Our list excludes the very large central cities since their circumstances regarding local tax and revenue problems may differ substantially from those of Atlanta. From the data in Table 6.2, it is clear that Atlanta is a good representative of these 20 cities.

From Table 6.2 it is obvious that, if reduction of the reliance on the property tax is a prime local finance objective in central cities, cities such as Indianapolis, Milwaukee, and Newark may find the results of the current case study of more immediate interest than even Atlanta, which relies much less on the property levy for local revenues. On the other hand, Atlanta is quite close to the mean level of population, income, and property tax reliance for these 20 cities.

Although Atlanta is a representative city with respect to the several characteristics shown in Table 6.2, the generality of the findings of our research likely rests much more on other socio-economic characteristics of the cities than on those characteristics reported in Table 6.2. For that reason, Table 6.3 has been constructed. Under the assumptions of the general-equilibrium model, two of the more important characteristics that would indicate the possibility of exporting taxes from the locality are the industrial composition of the local economic base and the patterns of commutation of the labor force within the city. More specifically, city taxes are more likely to be borne by nonresidents of the city if the industrial composition of the city is devoted relatively heavily to manufacturing and wholesaling activities or if much of the labor force working in the city resides outside.

From the first five columns of Table 6.3, we see that the proportion of employment within the sample of cities devoted to manufacturing and wholesaling ranges from 0.239 to 0.582 and 0.080 to 0.209,

TABLE 6.2

Demographic and Financial Characteristics of Selected Cities

City	(1) Population (in thou- sands)	(2) Income per Capita (dollars)	(3) Local Tax and License Revenues per Capita (dollars)	(4) Property Tax as Percent of Local Tax and License Revenues
Atlanta	497.0	3,163	92.20	58.5
Baltimore	905.8	2,886	221.78	73.4
Buffalo	469.8	2,963	141.00	91.9
Cincinnati	452.5	3,141	113.96	49.5
Dallas	844.4	3,737	105.76	68.5
Denver	514.7	3,557	136.44	46.9
Cleveland	750.9	2,849	127.41	58.8
Houston	1,232.8	3,395	82.42	63.7
Indianapolis	747.1	3,518	65.63	99.2
Kansas City (Mo.)	507.1	3,114	110.87	34.3
Miami	334.9	2,844	105.42	63.7
Milwaukee	717.1	3,204	92.93	96.3
Minneapolis	434.4	3,496	92.29	91.5
Newark	382.4	2,498	280.55	89.8
New Orleans	593.5	2,719	102.36	38.7
Pittsburgh	520.1	3,136	127.48	58.4
St. Louis	622.2	2,772	162.38	36.2
St. Paul	309.9	3,466	82.80	84.1
San Diego	696.8	3,533	62.72	54.0
San Jose	445.8	3,404	66.43	62.4
Mean	599.0	3,170	123.24	62.7

Sources: U. S. Bureau of the Census, Census of Population: 1970, vol. 1; U. S. Bureau of the Census, City Government Finances in 1969-70.

TABLE 6.3

Employment Characteristics
of Selected Cities
(in percent)

| City | City Employment by Industrial Sector | | | | | City-SMSA Comparisons | |
	Mfg.	Whole-sale	Retail	Serv.	Govt.	City Employ./ Suburban Pop.	City Retail SMSA Retail
Atlanta	30.6	20.9	27.0	17.7	3.7	50.7	72.0
Baltimore	42.1	10.1	22.3	11.0	14.6	36.8	54.2
Buffalo	53.7	13.2	22.8	11.3	10.2	44.9	41.8
Cincinnati	49.3	12.4	18.8	11.0	8.5	48.8	49.2
Cleveland	57.3	10.9	15.8	10.7	5.3	51.4	44.7
Dallas	43.3	16.3	23.0	13.6	3.8	a	a
Denver	45.3	15.2	22.3	12.3	4.9	a	a
Houston	37.3	16.8	26.8	15.8	3.3	22.2	77.2
Indianapolis	51.5	12.6	24.0	9.4	2.6	19.8	65.8
Kansas City (Mo.)	47.9	13.7	21.3	13.5	3.7	55.4	54.8
Miami	23.9	15.7	31.9	23.6	4.9	57.1	38.1
Milwaukee	55.1	9.8	21.4	9.2	4.5	30.4	61.2
Minneapolis	43.1	16.0	24.1	13.6	3.2	42.3	57.2
Newark	49.4	11.8	16.4	12.0	10.2	50.8	25.4
New Orleans	26.9	16.5	30.0	18.6	7.9	27.8	70.5
Pittsburgh	46.6	13.7	22.9	12.7	4.1	49.2	37.6
St. Louis	52.1	13.8	16.8	11.8	5.4	53.3	37.4
St. Paul	54.9	9.9	22.4	9.7	3.1	b	b
San Diego	40.0	8.0	28.9	18.5	4.6	26.4	56.6
San Jose	45.9	9.0	28.8	12.7	3.7	33.3	42.7
Total for the 20 cities	45.5	13.4	22.4	12.9	5.7	39.3	48.6

aNot computed, since SMSA includes other major city.
bIncluded in Minneapolis entry.

Sources: Employment data for 1967 from U. S. Bureau of the Census, Census of Manufacturing: 1967; U. S. Bureau of the Census, Census of Business: 1967; U. S. Bureau of the Census, Census of Governments: 1967. Population data for 1970 from U. S. Bureau of the Census, Census of Population: 1970, "Census Tracts."

respectively. Given that Atlanta is near the lower bound of the
first range and at the top of the second range, the exportability of
taxes as estimated in this study may not differ substantially from
the other cities in this list, taken as a group. (Note that 51.5
percent of Atlanta employment is in manufacturing and wholesale,
compared with 59.9 percent for the entire group of cities.)
However, when one considers cities individually, different
implications are likely to result. Thus, although Miami and New
Orleans appear to have low exportability of taxes via the wholesaling
and manufacturing sectors, their tourist attractiveness makes them
prime candidates for taxes such as hotel/motel excises and other
tourist-related levies. On the other hand, St. Louis and Kansas
City with their above-average proportion of employees in both
the manufacturing and wholesaling sectors are likely to export
a substantial portion of their taxes.

A second and certainly important aspect of the exporting question
concerns the residential location of the workers. Thus, to the
extent that workers in the central city reside in the suburbs, a
payroll tax may yield important revenues while being borne
primarily by nonresidents of the city. The sixth column of Table 6.3
sheds light on the relative importance of commuters into the central
city. The proportions shown there are the ratios of central-city
employees living in the SMSA but outside the central city to total
number of workers working in the central city and living anywhere
within the SMSA. Thus, higher ratios indicate relatively greater
levels of commutation into the central city. We see from these
data that Atlanta lies at the upper end of the range of values. The
cities of Miami and Kansas City would find exportation of payroll
taxes most possible from these data, while Indianapolis and Houston
are at the lower end of the range, thus indicating less likelihood
of ability to export payroll taxes. (Of course, in most cases the
power to tax is granted by the state, and, therefore, political
questions might arise as to whether such taxes are desirable.
Further, as we discuss below, our analysis assumed that suburban
areas do not simultaneously impose similar taxes.)

Another residence-location factor related to the suburban
exportability of central-city taxes concerns shopping patterns.
To the extent that persons live in the suburbs but shop within the
central city and pay taxes indirectly through forward-shifting,
such local taxes are exported. As a crude proxy measure of this
possibility over the cities listed in Table 6.3, we determined the
proportion of retail employment within the SMSA that is employed
within the central city. Here we see Atlanta standing near the
top of the list. Houston and New Orleans along with Atlanta
are most likely to be able to export taxes via retail sales, while
Newark, St. Louis, and Pittsburgh are least likely to do so.

In the above analysis, the exporting of the local income tax was shown to occur only via the federal tax offset and, further, was tied specifically to the Georgia state income tax. Exporting of this tax then would depend primarily upon its rate structure (on the structure of the tax in the state in which the city is located) and on the distribution of income within the city. Very unequal incomes together with a highly progressive local tax structure would allow for greater exporting since high-income persons would pay the primary burdens of the local tax but then could turn around and offset more of the local levy.

The incidence of the local taxes in the different cities could, of course, also differ from the results presented here; however, it is most likely that, using similar models and methodologies, income inequality would be altered in the same direction as was obtained in this monograph. Different compositions of renters and owners of residences could alter the findings with respect to the property tax, as would different institutional arrangements regarding assessment ratios and homestead exemptions. Different consumption patterns could lead to different results regarding the incidence of a local sales tax, as would institutional arrangements that allow for certain items to be exempt from the tax. Different sources of incomes—for example, transfers that are generally nontaxable or special provisions regarding capital gains—could also affect income tax incidence. Finally, as indicated above, since the federal tax offset is tied to a progressive federal tax structure, changes in income inequality net of federal offsets would themselves depend upon the income distribution within the city.

We, therefore, conclude that while this case study may not have explicit policy implications for all other central cities considering alternative taxes as a solution to their revenue problems, it is indicative of the types of effects likely to occur in other circumstances. Only more explicit case studies of the particular governmental units could derive more concrete conclusions.

EVALUATION AND FUTURE RESEARCH STRATEGY

While certain policy recommendations can be derived from this study, it is necessary to keep in mind several features of the research that make policy prescriptions less than certain. First, of course, the general methodological approach taken here relies upon the validity of a theoretical model and certain behavioral assumptions from which the results were drawn. To the extent that such assumptions or hypothesized relationships are vastly different from reality, the implications from the model may be in error. In

addition, since many of the empirical estimates had to be derived
from a variety of diverse data sources, some of which used different
definitions, the accuracy of the particular numbers generated may
be open to question. Finally, the analysis here has been one of
unilateral changes in local taxes and assumes no changes in the
tax structure of other localities.[1] Since this may not be possible
within the tax powers of localities granted by states, interdepen-
dencies of actions may alter the results obtained.

Regardless of these possible weaknesses or problems with the
analysis, the study has provided insight into answers of important
policy-related questions. In addition, from the study, it is
obvious that further work along these lines could further aid
policy-makers considering alternative taxes as local revenue sources.
Among these lines of research suggested from the current study are
the following:

1. Creation of a three-sector model so that land can be
included in the analysis explicitly.

2. Use of alternative factor mobility assumptions.

3. Allowance for interdependent taxing jurisdictions.

4. Obtaining of better estimates of the distributions of permanent
or normal incomes within the city.[2]

5. Since the major local tax is the property levy and since our
incidence analysis showed the crucial nature played by the demand
for housing in ascertaining its progressivity or regressivity,
additional knowledge of the income/housing relationship is
necessary.

6. This study has, of course, considered only taxes. The
total distributional effect of the city fisc can be determined only
after also considering the exporting and distributions of benefits
of local activities.

7. Since cities are generally different in numerous ways,
policy prescriptions derived from such studies are really only
feasible from a longer series of studies such as these.[3]

Of course, one would hope that such additional research would
emcompass at least several of the additional suggestions made
here so that our knowledge of local finance can truly be increased.
In this way, results may guide policy-makers to more intelligent
choices regarding local revenue sources.

NOTES

1. See Peter Mieszkowski, "The Property Tax: An Excise Tax
or a Profits Tax?" Journal of Public Economics 1 (1972): 73-96,
for a theoretical discussion of the differences between treating the
property tax as a local tax and as a uniform nationwide tax.

2. Dick Netzer, "The Incidence of the Property Tax Revisited," National Tax Journal 26 (1973): 515-33, argues that it may not be desirable to use permanent income because of the high geographic mobility.

3. Ibid. Netzer has called for such a series of studies.

Advisory Commission on Intergovernmental Relations. City Financial Emergencies: The Intergovernmental Dimension. Washington, D. C.: Government Printing Office, 1973.

——. Financing Schools and Property Tax Relief: A State Responsibility. Washington, D. C.: Government Printing Office, 1973.

——. Local Nonproperty Taxes and the Coordinating Role of the State. Washington, D. C.: Government Printing Office, 1961.

——. Public Opinion and Taxes. Washington, D. C.: Government Printing Office, 1972.

——. State-Local Finances: Significant Features and Suggested Legislation. Washington, D. C.: Government Printing Office, 1972.

——. "State-Local Revenue Systems and Education Finance." Unpublished report to the President's Commission on School Finance, November 12, 1971.

——. Urban America and the Federal System. Washington, D. C.: Government Printing Office, 1969.

Arizona Intergovernmental Structure: A Financial View to 1980. Phoenix: the Department, 1971.

Atlanta Constitution. "U. S. Cities Cut Services, Jobs to Make Ends Meet," November 29, 1974, p. 1.

Atlanta Department of Finance. 1970 Annual Report of the Director of Finance. Atlanta: the Department, 1971.

Atlanta Public Schools. 1969-70 Statistical Report. Atlanta, 1970.

Atlanta Regional Metropolitan Planning Commission. Housing All Atlantans: Subsidy Programs. Atlanta: the Commission, 1970.

Bahl, Roy. Metropolitan City Expenditures. Lexington: University of Kentucky Press, 1968.

Bradford, David; R. Malt; and Wallace Oates. "The Rising Cost of
    Local Public Service: Some Evidence and Reflections."
    National Tax Journal 22 (1969): 185-202.

Brazer, Harvey. City Expenditures in the United States. New York:
    National Bureau of Economic Research, 1959.

Break, George. "The Incidence and Economic Effects of Taxation."
    In The Economics of Public Finance, edited by Alan Binder,
    Robert Solow, et al. Washington, D. C.: Brookings Institution,
    1974, pp. 119-237.

Bridges, Benjamin, Jr. "The Elasticity of the Property Tax Base:
    Some Cross-Section Estimates." Land Economics 40 (1964):
    449-51.

Brittain, John A. The Payroll Tax for Social Security. Washington,
    D. C.: Brookings Institution, 1972.

Brown, Harry. "The Incidence of a General Output or a General
    Sales Tax." Journal of Political Economy 47 (1939): 254-62.

Brownlee, O. H. Estimated Distribution of Minnesota Taxes and
    Public Expenditure Benefits. Minneapolis: University of
    Minnesota Press, 1960.

Buchanan, James. Fiscal Theory and Political Economy. Durham:
    University of North Carolina Press, 1960.

Carliner, Geoffrey. "Income Elasticity of Housing Demand."
    Review of Economics and Statistics 55 (1973): 528-32.

Davies, David. "Financing Urban Functions and Services."
    In State and Local Finance, edited by William Mitchell and
    Ingo Walter. New York: Ronald Press, 1970.

———. "The Sensitivity of Consumption Taxes to Fluctuations in
    Income." National Tax Journal 15 (1962):281-90.

Donheiser, Alan. "The Incidence of the New York City Tax System."
    In Financing Government in New York City, edited by Dick
    Netzer. New York: New York University School of Public
    Administration, 1966.

Friedlaender, Ann, and John Due. "Tax Burden, Excess Burden and
    Differential Incidence Burden." Public Finance/Finances
    Publiques 27 (1972):312-23.

Georgia Department of Revenue. 1971 Statistical Report. Atlanta, 1971.

Gorman, John A. "The Relationship between Personal Income and Taxable Income." Survey of Current Business 50 (1970):19-21.

Harberger, Arnold. "The Incidence of the Corporation Income Tax." Journal of Political Economy 70 (1962):214-40.

Harberger, Arnold, and Martin Bailey. The Taxation of Income from Capital. Washington, D. C.: Brookings Institution, 1969, pp. 223-74.

Harris, Robert. Income and Sales Taxes: The 1970 Outlook for States and Localities. Chicago: Council of State Governments, 1966.

Harriss, C. Lowell. "Property Taxation: What's Good and What's Bad about It." Journal of Economics and Sociology 33 (1974): 89-102.

Heilbrun, James. Urban Economics and Public Policy. New York: St. Martin's Press, 1974.

Hirsch, Werner. "Fiscal Plight: Causes and Remedies." In Hirsch et al., Fiscal Pressures on the Central City. New York: Praeger Publishers, 1971.

Hirsch, Werner et al. Fiscal Pressures on the Central City. New York: Praeger Publishers, 1971.

Internal Revenue Service. Statistics of Income—1969, Individual Income Tax Returns. Washington, D. C.: Government Printing Office, 1971.

King, Irene. Bond Sales for Public School Purposes, 1970-71. Washington, D. C.: U. S. Office of Education, National Center for Educational Statistics, 1972.

Lee, T. N. "Housing and Permanent Income: Tests Based on a Three-Year Reinterview Survey." Review of Economics and Statistics 50 (1968):480-90.

deLeeuw, Frank. "The Demand for Housing: A Review of Cross-Section Evidence." Review of Economics and Statistics 53 (1971):1-10.

Lucas, Robert. "Labor-Capital Substitution in U. S. Manufacturing."
    In The Taxation of Income from Capital, edited by Arnold
    Harberger and Martin Bailey. Washington, D. C.: Brookings
    Institution, 1969.

McLoone, Eugene P. "Effects of Tax Elasticities on the Financial
    Support of Education." Unpublished Ph.D. dissertation,
    College of Education, University of Illinois, 1961.

McLure, Charles. "The Interstate Exporting of State and Local
    Taxes: Estimates for 1962." National Tax Journal 20 (1967):49-77.

————. "The Inter-Regional Incidence of General Regional Taxes."
    Public Finance/Finances Publiques 24 (1969):457-83.

————. "Taxation, Substitution and Industrial Location." Journal of
    Political Economy 78 (1970):112-32.

————. "The Theory of Tax Incidence with Imperfect Factor Mobility."
    Finanzarchiv 30 (1970):27-48.

Maisel, S. J.; J. B. Burnham; and J. S. Austin. "The Demand for
    Housing: A Comment." Review of Economics and Statistics 53
    (1971):410-13.

Mieszkowski, Peter. "Tax Incidence Theory: The Effects of Taxes
    on the Distribution of Income." Journal of Economic Literature 7
    (1969):1103-24.

————. "On the Theory of Tax Incidence." Journal of Political
    Economy 75 (1967):250-62.

————. "The Property Tax: An Excise or a Profits Tax?" Journal
    of Public Economics 1 (1972):73-96.

Musgrave, Richard. "On Incidence." Journal of Political Economy 61
    (1953):308-23.

————. The Theory of Public Finance. New York: McGraw-Hill,
    1959.

————; and Darwin Daicoff. "Who Pays the Michigan Tax."
    Michigan Tax Study, Staff Papers. Lansing, Mich., 1958.

————et al. "Distribution of Tax Payments by Income Groups:
    A Case Study for 1948." National Tax Journal 4 (1951):1-53.

Mushkin, Selma. Property Taxes: The 1970 Outlook. Chicago:
    Council of State Governments, 1965.

Nation's Cities. "City Taxes and Services" (August 1971):10-22.

Netzer, Richard. "Financial Needs and Resources over the Next
    Decade." In Public Finances: Needs, Sources and Utilization.
    Princeton, N. J.: Princeton University Press, 1961.

——. Impact of the Property Tax: Its Economic Implications for
    Urban Problems. U. S. Congress, Joint Economic Committee
    and the National Commission on Urban Problems. Washington,
    D. C.: Government Printing Office, 1968.

——. "The Incidence of the Property Tax Revisited." National
    Tax Journal 26 (1973):515-36.

Peck, John E. "Financing State Expenditures in a Prospering Economy."
    Indiana Business Review 64 (1969):7-15.

Peterson, George E. "The Regressivity of the Residential Property
    Tax." Journal of Public Economics (forthcoming).

Rafuse, Robert W. "Cyclical Behavior of State-Local Finances."
    In Essays in Fiscal Federalism, edited by Richard A. Musgrave.
    Washington, D. C.: Brookings Institution, 1965.

Recktenwald, Horst. Tax Incidence and Income Redistribution.
    Detroit: Wayne State University Press, 1971.

Reischauer, Robert, and Robert Hartman. Reforming School Finance.
    Washington, D. C.: Brookings Institution, 1973.

Rolph, Earl. "A Proposed Revision of Excise-Tax Theory."
    Journal of Political Economy 60 (1952):102-17.

Ruggles, Richard. "The Federal Government and Federalism."
    In Revenue Sharing and the City, edited by Harvey Perloff
    and Richard Nathan. Baltimore: Johns Hopkins Press, 1968.

Sacks, Seymour, and John Callahan. "Central City-Suburban Fiscal
    Disparities in the 72 Largest Metropolitan Areas." In Advisory
    Commission on Intergovernmental Relations, City Financial
    Emergencies. Washington, D. C.: Government Printing Office,
    1973, pp. 91-152.

Schroeder, L. D.; W. Sheftall; and D. L. Sjoquist. "Variations in Property Tax Assessment Ratios: The Case of Fulton County." Atlanta Economic Review (forthcoming).

Sjoquist, David L., and Larry D. Schroeder. "A Method for Constructing Distributions of Broad-based Income for Metropolitan Areas and Central Cities." Unpublished Working Paper 7374-04, revised January 1974. Atlanta: Department of Economics, Georgia State University, 1974.

Terrell, Henry S. "The Fiscal Impact of Nonwhites." In Hirsch et al., Fiscal Pressures on the Central City. New York: Praeger Publishers, 1971.

U. S. Bureau of Labor Statistics. "Consumer Expenditures and Income Cross-Classification of Family Characteristics (Urban United States), 1960-1961." Survey of Consumer Expenditures, BLS-Report 237-38, Supplement 2-Part A. Washington, D. C.: Government Printing Office, 1964.

———. "Government Work Stoppages, 1960, 1969 and 1970," 1971; processed.

———. Work Stoppages in Government, 1958-68, Report 34. Washington, D. C.: Government Printing Office, 1970.

U. S. Bureau of the Census. Census of Business, 1967, vol. 2, Retail Trade-Area Statistics; vol. 4, Wholesale Trade-Area Statistics; vol. 5, Selected Services-Area Statistics. Washington, D. C.: Government Printing Office, 1970.

———. Census of Governments: 1967. Washington, D. C.: Government Printing Office, 1968.

———. Census of Housing: 1970, Metropolitan Housing Characteristics, Final Report HC(2)-15 Atlanta, GA SMSA. Washington, D. C.: Government Printing Office, 1972.

———. Census of Manufacturing, 1967, vol. 2, Area Statistics. Washington, D. C.: Government Printing Office, 1971.

———. Census of Population: 1970 General Social and Economic Characteristics, Final Report PC(1). Washington, D. C.: Government Printing Office, 1972.

———. Census of Population and Housing: 1970, Census Tracts, Final Report PHC(1)-14 Atlanta, GA SMSA. Washington, D. C.: Government Printing Office, 1972.

——. City Government Finances in 1969-70. Washington, D. C.: Government Printing Office, 1971.

——. County Business Patterns: 1970, Georgia CBP-70-12. Washington, D. C.: Government Printing Office, 1971.

____. Current Population Reports, Series P-60, No. 75, "Income in 1969 of Families and Persons in the United States." Washington, D. C.: Government Printing Office, 1970.

——. Local Government Finance in Selected Metropolitan Areas and Large Counties: 1969-70 and 1971-72. Washington, D. C.: Government Printing Office, 1971, 1974.

——. 1970 Census Users' Guide. Washington, D. C.: Government Printing Office, 1970.

U. S. Department of Commerce, Office of Business Economics. "Personal Income in Metropolitan and Non-Metropolitan Areas." Survey of Current Business 51 (1971):16-32.

ABOUT THE AUTHORS

LARRY D. SCHROEDER is Assistant Professor of Economics, Georgia State University. He earned his B. A. at Central College, Iowa, his M. A. at Northern Illinois University, and his Ph. D. at the University of Wisconsin, Madison.

DAVID L. SJOQUIST is Associate Professor of Economics, Georgia State University. He received his B. A. at the College of St. Thomas, and his M. A. and Ph. D. at the University of Minnesota.

Both authors have published articles in journals of economics and sociology.

TAXES, EXPENDITURES AND THE ECONOMIC
BASE: Case Study of New York City
Roy W. Bahl, Alan K. Campbell, and
David Greytak

URBAN INCENTIVE TAX CREDITS:
A Self-Correcting Strategy to Rebuild
Central Cities
Edward M. Meyers and John J. Musial

PERSPECTIVES ON TAX REFORM: Death Taxes,
Tax Loopholes, and the Value Added Tax
Richard E. Wagner, Roger A. Freeman,
Charles E. Mclure Jr., Norman B. Ture,
and Eric Schiff

TAXES ON DIRECT INVESTMENT INCOME
IN THE EEC: A Legal and Economic Analysis
Bernard Snoy

REAL PROPERTY TAXATION IN NEW YORK CITY
Phillip Finklestein